YOUR HOLIDAY HOME

Canadian holiday home sited to inspire escapists everywhere

YOUR
HOLIDAY HOME

AUDREY POWELL

DAVID & CHARLES
NEWTON ABBOT

0 7153 5436 1

Set in eleven on thirteen point Baskerville
and printed in Great Britain
by W J Holman Limited Dawlish
for David & Charles (Publishers) Limited
South Devon House Newton Abbot Devon

Contents

List of Illustrations

PLATES

CHAPTER 1

Why a holiday home?

The holiday home market is a growing one.

It began expanding in the fifties as people took to snapping up country cottages as weekend places and has never looked back. That much is certain. But the number of properties actually involved and the rate at which second-home owning is increasing is by no means agreed. Of estimates there are plenty: but facts are few.

The Department of the Environment has become interested in the subject and is having market research figures fed to it.

The Countryside Commission has had a survey on second-home ownership carried out by a team from Wye College, University of London. They talked to owners in Essex, Devon, the Lake District and Wales, and sent them intriguing questionnaires asking, among other things, what activities they engaged in while at their second homes.

The Commission, conscious of the rapid growth of holiday homes in Europe and North America, and foreseeing a possible surge of purpose-built holiday homes in this country when the cottages run out, wants a policy formulated for properly planned development in this sphere.

There was originally a question in the 1971 census on second-home ownership but it came out. This was a pity, because some countries use this means of getting accurate figures. But here, statistics to support the general agreement that second-home ownership is building up, are lacking.

Part of the problem is in defining second homes. Do you include caravans and houseboats? What about families who live in the country and have a *pied á terre* in London or whose second home is abroad?

Estimates of second homes range from 100,000 to 400,000 —but some relate to England and Wales, others to the whole of Britain.

There is a similar variation in assessments of demand. This has been suggested as from 10,000 to 30,000 a year by different sources. But how much would require new building, how much be absorbed by old places becoming vacant?

Long term figures are equally at variance. There have been all sorts of estimates up to nearly 2,000,000 for the number of second homes likely to be owned by the British by the end of the century. Obviously the subject will keep researchers busy for a long time to come.

In Scandinavia and North America a holiday home is a normal possession for a great many families and, like the second car, it could become an important market in Britain too. How much this market will in fact grow depends on how incomes increase and working hours decrease, on the availability and price of suitable property, and on whether building societies may need to find new outlets for money and builders new ways of stimulating demand for housing. On the other hand, the reduction of air fares might attract people abroad more often and lessen the demand for second homes in Britain.

It is surprising, even now, how many of one's friends turn out to have a weekend cottage in Wales, a bungalow on the east coast, or an apartment in Majorca. Sometimes these holiday homes are just happy-go-lucky chalet affairs that nobody makes any fuss about owning, but they give adults a break and children a lot of pleasure.

About 20 per cent of French families own or have the use of holiday homes, many inherited and in the country, some newly built on the Mediterranean coast. In Sweden nearly half a million households have holiday homes and the number is increasing by 28,000 a year. It is often just four walls and a roof in the forest or by the water, but the family make good use of it. Wife and children will go there for most of the summer, and the husband spend his holiday and weekends there. In Denmark, too, about 138,500 families have holiday homes, and a large number of Norwegians have their hut in the mountains or down by the fjords.

About a third of the population of Finland have a summer home, perhaps the family house in the country, no longer lived in permanently as younger generations move into flats in town, but used in turn by branches of the family for vacations. Or the second home may be by a lakeside, a cabin built for about £2,200 and sleeping four or five. It will always have its sauna, in fact the sauna may come first, with the minimum of other accommodation. The cabin will be extended later, as money becomes available, to make room for extra family and friends.

Often these homes are electrically heated and used as winter skiing chalets as well. Sometimes the heating can be switched on by remote control from a nearby village and the owner has an arrangement with a villager to do this when telephoned, so that the cabin is warm on arrival.

In Canada you begin to feel that almost everyone has a second home. In one office in Ottawa, seven out of nine stenographers had their holiday cottages. With cities so hot in summer, the cottage by the lake or on high ground is in almost continual use from May onwards by wife, children and grandparents, with husbands commuting at weekends. Here, too, many of the cottages are used as winter sports bases.

Canadian building of second homes is rising by about 50 per cent a year. The largest portion of the increase is in pre-fabricated cottages or pre-cut packages in western red cedar, with the ever-popular A-frame—'a solid little take-off from a tent'—as the overall sales leader.

Manufacturers of pre-cut pre-engineered shells, or of complete do-it-yourself packages, or builder-erected packages, are all vying for a share of the growing market. One Canadian manufacturer who specialises in do-it-yourself packages at under £1,640 is expecting a 75 per cent increase in sales in the coming year. But as land prices rise there is increased interest in higher priced designs.

There is also a growth in the number of architect-designed and custom-built homes by vacation specialists. These are often planned as retirement homes—'the dream home in the dream location'—the dream location being far removed from the labour market, as one Canadian said. These may be built in stages and used first for holidays. Again cedar is popular as it costs little to maintain and fits into the landscape.

Across the Atlantic they really go to town with their 'getaway homes', or 'escape hatches', and produce a spectrum of types and designs that make the British cottage/bungalow/flat selection seem woefully unimaginative. They will sell you saltboxes, crow's nests, cluster cabins or treehouses; bi-, tri-, or multi-levels; round houses, 'hillsides', or atriums; Dutch colonials, Bavarians or add-a-units, for your 'lakeside haven', for 'living embraced by nature', or for 'the retreat where problems just dissolve'.

An American magazine devoted entirely to the subject of vacation homes, says with some truth that perhaps 'the saddest commentary on the tempo of modern life is the longing to get away from it'.

So they do the getting away in a style that makes the British look as if they haven't even tried.

As the standard of living rises in Britain we can expect the second-home cult to grow. And although this may seem a luxury to people whose only homes leave a lot to be desired, it is not necessarily so.

Much of the increase in second-home owning is due to the crowded conditions of city life. Londoners with children, forced for lack of an alternative to live in unsuitable flats, can hardly be blamed for giving the youngsters the freedom of a cottage with a garden at weekends. The noise of neighbours' TV and transistors have driven other families to seek the solitude of a weekend cottage.

Those who live close to airports—or even miles away but in the flight paths of jets—certainly need a little quietness at some time. In a similar situation are the many who now find themselves on motorways or heavily used roads. Indeed, anyone who breathes the fumes of a big city night and day surely has a case for getting some clean air by the coast or in the country at weekends.

With a home outside the city he can at least cut out some of the wasted hours in weekend traffic jams, and he and the family can get the benefit of a change at times when crowds or doubtful weather might make them abandon an outing that involved looking for picnic spots.

Longer holidays have had much to do with the growth of second-home owning. A couple of weeks in an hotel or guesthouse is fine, but more can be boring and too expensive for the average family. Yet the alternative of spending the rest of the time at home seems a waste. So some sort of simple leisure home is a satisfactory compromise. Mother and children can spend all the school holidays there and the rest of the family use it when they are free.

There are other points in favour of a holiday home. Not least is the continual rise in the value of property, which makes something like a well-sited country cottage a good investment.

It can be argued that in this way the town dweller is pushing up prices for local people. But often the locals have little interest in the tumbledown cottages that delight weekenders, and want something new and labour saving. In some instances the townsman who buys a cottage for his sparetime enjoyment saves it from being left to crumble away. This is also an answer to those who say he should not be using improvement grants to help restore the property.

The 'anti' lobby say that second-home owners leave villages dead in winter; the 'pros' say they bring trade to jobbing builders and, particularly if they let to tenants who are there all the week, to shopkeepers.

Some second-home buyers are people planning ahead for retirement. The longer they put off buying their bungalow or cottage the more they will have to pay. If they get it early they can improve and equip it on full income, and work on the property and garden while still active. They also avoid the sudden switch from one area and one way of life to another. Many a couple who retire to the coast or the country after a life in town are soon back looking for a home among the familiar city sounds and shops. They find the complete change too much. But owning a place several years before retirement gives them a chance to get to know it in winter as well as summer; to make friends among shopkeepers and neighbours, and to begin to become part of the community.

14

It sometimes happens that people who buy a second home simply for holidays and with no thought of retiring to it, later do so, because through regular visits they have become attached to the area.

On the other side of the coin are those who don't find the project the fun they thought it would be. They learn that restoring an old place amounts to rather more than they bargained for, and it also runs into a lot more money. Most country agents can produce half-renovated cottages, back on the market.

Some families find a second home a solution to the three-generation problem. An elderly parent may be settled happily in one in a village or by the sea, with a neighbour keeping an eye on him. During the week he can enjoy his independence and know that he is doing a useful job as caretaker of the cottage and perhaps keeping the garden trim. At weekends the family come down to be with him and give the children a change from town life. But young and old are not together long enough for tiffs to develop.

Or a second home can be acquired simply as a hobby— by a couple whose town flat would not lend itself to experiments in decoration, nor would their landlord approve. One woman who liked refurnishing her main house at intervals resented almost having to give away the unwanted stuff and found using it to furnish a holiday cottage an ideal solution.

A family, living in a popular area found life getting more and more expensive as relatives and friends turned up uninvited each weekend and expected to be entertained. So the family decided on a simple solution, which did not offend anyone, and took themselves off to an out-of-the-way spot, from Fridays to Mondays.

Some buy holiday homes as a straightforward investment and can do quite well out of it. Some let occasionally when they do not want the place themselves, and this may or may not prove a good idea.

There is a growing section who have bought their holiday home abroad, so that they can have the sun, cheap wine and cigarettes, with all the other attractions, more often than if they had to pay hotel bills for the family every time they went out of the country.

In this country at present, houses and cottages account for more than half the second homes, and bungalows and chalets for most of the rest, along with caravans. But with the cottage type of property getting scarcer, newly built holiday home colonies in the Scandinavian style will presumably make their appearance in due course.

Meantime the agents rub their hands with delight whenever a convertible cottage turns up.

However, in spite of all the advice that is handed out about turning a cowshed into a glossy-magazine-type weekend home, I have more than a suspicion that a large number of families who acquire a country hideaway don't work themselves to death on it. 'We want to get the feel of the place first', they say. And two years later they haven't finished painting the living room. It may be just a ploy to keep visitors away.

They don't all go haring up mountainsides and rushing round taking healthy exercise, either. If you ask many how they spend their time they simply seem to sit and relax. What they wanted, it appears, was just a change of scene. But a high proportion seem to have gardens of some sort. So they either like gardening, or they like looking at weeds.

Page 17 Traditional cottages: *(above)* period cottage in West Sussex before conversion; *(below)* this one was in similar disrepair

Page 18 *(above)* Away from it all but not out of the modern stream: modern holiday home, also suitable for retirement, at Brixham; *(below)* modern Guildway cottage

CHAPTER 2

For and against

There are plenty of snags in owning two homes, apart from double lots of rates, electricity, gas, telephone and other bills. You would do well to budget this carefully before embarking on a 'double life'.

By no means everyone finds that the idea works out. Many give up their second property after a few years because of the cost, or the travelling, or because they were not making enough use of it. Most people seem to think three hours is enough to spend in travelling to a weekend lair; certainly the nearer it is the more you are likely to use it. Bear in mind that you may be on the road when it is most congested, and that you will want to be at your second home just when the garden at your main one is at its best.

Some people have found it wasn't worth the worry, with neighbours ringing up in winter saying pipes had burst and water was running out under the door, or tiles had come off and rain was pouring in. Or they found it was getting damp or deteriorating through lack of use, or being broken into. If for a run of weekends one or two members of the family have something interesting to do in town,

B

weeks can go by with the cottage unused.

Other owners have found it too complicated to have duplicates of everything, or that vital items were always in the other house. They got tired of packing and unpacking; perhaps carrying everything up and down in the lift at their block of flats.

If a cottage is too primitive the novelty of getting water from a pump umpteen times a day and having to heat it up may soon wear off. Having to dust, air beds and deal with the encroaching jungle of the garden can soon turn the holiday weekend into a chore unless you are able to arrange for a villager to come in beforehand and get things organised. But the locals, for their part, may resent a stranger who buys a place in their midst, only appears at intervals and doesn't bother much about the upkeep of the house and garden.

Some hardworking owners have found the glowing stories of profits made on selling a renovated place exaggerated. One owner dropped £7,000 on the sale of an expensively converted windmill. If you plan to get an income from your cottage, hoped for lettings may not materialise, or if they do, tenants may wreck the place or disappear without paying the rent. Or friends may continually be asking to borrow your hideaway for nothing, and not bother to replace the crockery they break.

Another snag with a holiday home is that if you are to make full use of it you will spend all your vacations in the same place—unless you do some swopping round with acquaintances who have similar properties.

One woman with a second home in Ireland exchanged it one year through the *Home Interchange Directory* (19 Bolton Street, Piccadilly, London W1). The swop was with an owner who had a similar home in Scotland, but she could have been more ambitious and possibly arranged to exchange her holiday home for a flat in New York or a house in Italy or the West Indies. It costs £4 to have your home listed in the Directory and from your own copy of it you get in touch with any owners with whom you would like to exchange.

There are some firms who sell overseas apartments on a system whereby an owner can lease back his property and be able to holiday in similar accommodation elsewhere—perhaps in another country—rent free, or at concessionary rates. Of course the overseas world has its own set of snags, including the dollar premium you have to add on if you buy out of the sterling area, and the different legal arrangements. But more of that in chapter 11.

I have found it interesting to talk to second-home owners and hear their experiences. A London literary agent, for example, with a house on the south coast uses it for some weekends and at other times lets it through an agency. It is large, detached, and sleeps eight. The agents ask from £24.50 to £60.50 a week for it, depending on the time of year. Most lettings come in the high season and are for a fortnight or month. Gas, electricity and laundry are included. Telephone calls are extra and there is a £25 returnable deposit. The agents ask the owner to state what rent is required and add their fee to this so that it is included in the amount paid by the tenant.

Getting help for cleaning is a difficulty encountered by this owner and many others. She finds she has to do the cleaning herself before she hands the house over, and expects her tenants to leave the place in a similar condition. She is there to meet new people when they arrive and tries to make the house look pleasant with flowers to welcome them—'Red, white and blue for some of my French visitors', she laughs.

21

This owner has been letting for ten years and has not had any bad experiences, although tenants vary considerably. 'Children occasionally draw on walls, and people who break things sometimes do not even admit it to each other so that some breakages do not get replaced.' She believes that if a property looks attractive and homelike people are less likely to knock it about. 'If it looks as if everything is just to let and anything will do, that is an open invitation not to take much care.'

Often her tenants are British people on leave from engagements abroad, perhaps oil families. Some have rented for two years running. Usually the tenants are of one family, perhaps husband and wife, children and in-laws, with an au pair.

One thing she has learned is that people are great at putting things away in wrong places. Time and again she wonders what is missing, 'but I keep calm and gradually the things all turn up'.

A Cornish housewife has a bungalow in her garden, and this she lets while she and her husband live in the main house. The bungalow sleeps seven—but she says she doesn't mind how many come as long as they leave the place as they find it. She has been letting it (latterly through an agency) for over fifteen years, one family from Scotland rented it for holidays for nine years in succession.

Here, too, cleaning help is hard to find. She and the tenants have to do this. 'I show them round when they arrive and usually have a chat with them each day, and let them have vegetables from the garden if they want them .I generally keep everything on a friendly basis and hope they have a good holiday.'

The bungalow has 'ordinary' furniture, she says—not particularly up to date, but with oak bedroom suites and built-in wardrobes. She provides electric kettle, iron and fridge. Electricity is on a meter. She charges £6.50 a week off-season for long lets and up to £24.50 a week in August —which includes the agent's charge. The bungalow is usually let for eight or nine weeks in a year and she would like to do more letting if she could.

The majority of her tenants are careful and leave everything in good condition. 'If they break something some will stick it together; others will say "How much?".' The money brought in through letting is useful, but part has, of course, to be used for doing the bungalow up.

An Ulster family chose their holiday house at the foot of the Mountains of Mourne, partly for its view and partly because it can be reached in an hour from their permanent home and so regular use can be made of it. It is a modern semi, too small for much entertaining. But this, they feel, is not a disadvantage; friends are told they can borrow the whole house when the owners do not want it, but they have to look after themselves.

The owners use it at weekends through the summer and for the whole of July and August, and find it lets easily in winter. They think winter letting is a good arrangement as it ensures that the house is supervised during this period. They do not seek the highest rent but concentrate on getting suitable tenants. An agent finds these, and his commission is based on an original system of letting for guineas and paying the owners in pounds. He reads the electric meter (there is no gas) when a tenant takes over and leaves, and holds a deposit. The family feel they have been fortunate with tenants; there has been no damage in spite of the fact that two tenants had four children each.

The garden has been made as labour-saving as possible, with grass, shrubs and roses. The owners prune the roses in the autumn and cut the grass before handing over to the winter tenant. Little attention is then needed until spring. During the summer half an hour with a motor mower at weekends deals with the lawn.

Each year they try to do something to improve the place and have added a water heater, sink unit, extractor fan and off-peak storage heating. They say that other people in the area, whose houses only have the bare essentials can get summer lettings, but do not find it so easy to let in winter.

A Surrey resident bought a period terrace cottage in Sussex for his second home. With three children he found it expensive to go abroad for holidays, so now he and his wife and children stay at the cottage for a fortnight in spring, three weeks in autumn and, if it is not let, at Christmas. Sometimes they weekend there as well.

His agents ask £9.50 a week from November to March and £37 a week for July, August and September. Rent includes central heating in winter. Light is on a meter. The cottage sleeps four adults and three children and the owners stipulate that there are to be no children under three years, no pets and no single week lettings in the high season. A £10 deposit is taken.

The cottage is in an area where it is not difficult to let from June to October continuously, and quite a lot at other times of the year as well. A number of the tenants come from overseas and want the house for three or four months —they are often people attached to international companies or in the diplomatic service. The British who take it are mostly professional people. The only unhappy experience they had was when they let to a schoolmaster who was found to have seven hippies staying with him as well. They smashed the electric meter.

At first the family used to let it themselves but found it

was simpler doing it through agents, who had 'everything worked out'. There is nothing to stop them letting it themselves whenever they wish. The key is left with a nearby grocer, whose name and address are on an information sheet sent to tenants in advance. He and a neighbour keep an eye on the place when it is vacant.

'If you want to borrow from a building society to buy a second home you must stress that you want to use it yourself and that it is not exclusively for letting,' says this owner. 'If you are going to live there even for only a short while in the year, then it is a holiday home. This is very important if you do not want the society to veto the whole idea.'

Even allowing for the cost of a mortgage and capital gains tax, it is a worthwhile investment he feels, when rent, tax relief on mortgages and capital appreciation are taken into account. It also provides a holiday base for the whole family, which is worth a good deal. And if you are going to live there in retirement you are already making a circle of friends there before you settle.

One point he makes is that when you have spent money and time improving a place like this it exerts a pull over you. It is not the relaxing thing you might assume. 'If it is empty you keep wondering all the time if it is all right and you want to be going to look at it. I have a friend with a similar place in Ireland. He says he has to go over four or five times a year for this reason. It costs him £60 each time with the family.'

A man living in a London flat with his wife and two children bought a weekend cottage in Suffolk. It was five miles from a station, and cheap. They did a lot of the modernising themselves, slowly, and with some help from an improvement grant. The rates are low and they don't find the running expenses of a second home very heavy. But it proves simpler for the wife and children to drive from home with whatever is needed for each weekend and the husband to go direct from his office by train. The same routine is followed at the end of the stay and these rail fares are a big item.

They furnished the cottage locally, from village second-hand shops and markets, and found this an amusing and cheap way of doing things. In all, they encountered fewer snags than they expected and the project also turned out to be less expensive than they expected. It gets them and he children into the country regularly, and they feel that it is one of the best things they have done.

A woman and her psychoanalyst husband living on the fringe of London bought a cottage in Wiltshire about three years ago because she liked living in the country and her husband's job tied him to town. He worked long hours so daily commuting to the country was out. They wanted a larger garden for their three children as well.

They decided to make a distance of eighty miles from their permanent home their limit. They had been used to visiting a relative farther away and felt a three hours' drive on Friday and Sunday evenings would be too much. As it is they can leave at 7.30 pm and have a meal, if they wish, in the other property at 9.30 pm. 'We drew a line taking in areas north-west, west and south-west of London, within our radius, and began looking.'

Some villages they eliminated right away because of the number of commuters there and because they did not offer enough change. A contributory factor to their buying of the Wiltshire property was that it was in a village 'just about as far from the sea as you can get', which made it cheaper. 'Everybody else was struggling to be within reach of the coast.'

They put their name down with five or six agents and while going through a village in search of another cottage, noticed one with thatch and a lot of nettles, in about one-third of an acre. It had a derelict For Sale sign up, and had obviously been empty for a long time.

They wrote to the agents named on the board: 'typically they hadn't given us details although it met all our requirements'. In fact it was two cottages and something like £3,500 was being asked for the pair, but eventually about £2,500 was agreed. 'We had to pay another £1,500 out on repairs in addition to an improvement grant.'

They had the thatch patched up, but are aware that it will need renewing in a few years at a cost of £800-£1,000 for the roofs of the two cottages—'we may buy shingles and remove the thatch'. They put in a bathroom and larder and repaired rotted flooring and put down tiles. There was a lot of damp and one wall was bulging in an ominous way, so that had to be dealt with. They are still redecorating.

At first they lived in the smaller and sounder of the two cottages, while working on the larger, but have now made the two into one. 'We slaved away most of the time on the garden, trying to make it presentable. I spent a lot of time weeding, but it is mostly grass. We bought a motor mower and grass cutting takes about two hours.'

They go to the cottage about three weekends out of four in summer and once a fortnight in the early part of the autumn. They also spend summer and Easter holidays there. But they do not find it worthwhile going in winter. The place tends to get damp since they cannot afford to leave heaters on, and they have to drain the tank for safety —too big a job to do frequently.

A village woman comes in to light heaters before they arrive, and cleans up after they go. 'I do not know how we could manage without her.' Neighbours also keep an eye on the property and report on it during the winter. This is the advantage of having a second home in a village instead of the usual dreamed-of isolated spot.

They collected furniture from various sources. A table had been left by the previous owner; they had had one spare bed and a friend had given them another; they had someone else's old fridge. They did buy a new cooker and had certain basic expenses, but furnishing was sparse, with mats and wooden chairs.

They had not let the cottage yet, as it was not ready, though they thought they might later. But they had let their London house while holidaying in the cottage, and that had worked out well. The main snag for them with second-home owning was that it was a tie—yet one more lot of bricks and mortar to look after. With the cottage and their London home there were seventeen rooms to keep decorated. One got tired. The result was that the main house did not get the attention it should and was, they said, 'gradually beginning to fall apart'. Another disadvantage was that two evenings a week were taken up in travelling, and this left less time for seeing friends.

On the credit side, the second home fulfilled its purpose of giving the children a garden to run around in. The family also got to know an entirely different type of people in the village, which was refreshing. If during the winter there was talk of selling the cottage, as soon as they went down for the first time in the spring 'there were the open skies, no aircraft, cows to look at . . . we would miss it, I think. With the sun shining and the daffodils coming out, on the whole I think it is worth it.'

It is amusing to try to decide what type of people own a second home, but in fact they can be anyone. In Britain as in most countries, a certain percentage have inherited cottages from relatives and kept them. As for the rest, second-home owning is by no means a prerogative of the rich, although having money to spare naturally helps. It seems to be more related to people's ability to make frequent use of a leisure property—not necessarily their amount of free time, but their freedom to arrange it to give themselves specially long weekends or a good slice of off-duty days. One new holiday site I visited had four doctors, three publicans, one pilot and one roadsweeper (who paid cash) among the early buyers of properties there.

If there is such a thing as an average buyer, he could be a family man, with several children, somewhere round forty, probably professional or in a hire-and-fire grading, with a reasonable salary but not necessarily on the top scale, and able to juggle his working hours round a bit.

CHAPTER 3

The sordid subject of finance

Raising the cash to buy a holiday home could be the point on which the whole exercise hinges. On the other hand, some people buy as a way of utilising spare capital, knowing the value of their property is almost bound to increase, sometimes spectacularly if it is just beyond the outer fringe of a city or a few miles from a projected motorway.

Some buyers are people who have just paid off a mortgage on a main house and feel able to continue payment on another. Building societies will tell you they don't often lend on second homes, or allow two mortgages. But things are not always what they seem—or as the official literature makes out. There are societies who will lend, and when money is flush quite a number do. It just means shopping around to find them, although you cannot hope for much in the tightest part of a credit squeeze.

'So much depends on the state of the market', said a mortgage broker. 'Buying a second home on mortgage when you are already making repayments on another has to be very carefully arranged and one must make sure double repayments are not over the top... It may mean pushing the proposition round the market and seeing if anybody is feeling kind-hearted, or sufficiently free with funds.'

While societies may officially shy off lending on second homes on the grounds that they are only in business to provide the family house, it is a subject that some of their officers have discussed publicly from time to time. For as the housing situation improves and demand for their money slackens in that direction, they will have to find further outlets. If you feel like contacting a few societies—and there are hundreds of them—you can find names and addresses in the *Building Societies' Year Book* in your public library. Or get a copy of the monthly *Building Societies' Gazette*, which has a directory of societies in each issue.

If you already own one house outright and simply want to borrow from a society for the weekend home, it is very much a question of having a connection with such a society, either through investment or through having had a previous mortgage from them, according to a building society official. It should not be too difficult in normal times.

'It is the idea of running two mortgages that is harder to talk them into—but not impossible, if your funds will stand it', he said. 'The small local societies are worth trying. They may charge slightly more, but they do tend to be flexible.'

Get your bank manager or solicitor to ask any societies they have connections with, or to whom they have given investment business, if they will help. Goodwill has a lot to do with it. If a request were to be made from such a quarter at a time when they had money in hand, a society might feel it good policy to be helpful.

'Basically the same principles apply as for an ordinary mortgage for the family home—security, with status', said another mortgage broker. 'And it depends on how much money they have. It is surprising how they forget objections when they have plenty of funds.'

31

An important consideration is that of letting. A society would be anxious to make certain of vacant possession should foreclosure be necessary and that any occupants of the second home had no security of tenure. Normally holiday letting of a bungalow or weekend cottage should not create a tenancy. 'If it is only let for odd weeks during the summer that is all right from their point of view,' said this same broker. But with longer lets, he admitted that you could run into problems, and that is why some people prefer to let through agents who know—or ought to know—how to avoid any difficulties arising through tenants refusing to leave.

There were times when the middle-sized building societies found it difficult to attract money, he went on, so they had to pay slightly more to investors and charge slightly more to borrowers. They were worth approaching for loans on second homes since they tended to get and to consider the more unusual types of application.

Some people seem to have the idea that building societies will not lend on older properties even in straightforward cases where a buyer has no other mortgage. Probably this impression goes back to times when money was tight and societies became more selective. But when there is no financial squeeze there should be no difficulty in getting a mortgage on an older place that is in reasonable repair. The Building Societies' Association, which represents more than 98 per cent of building society assets, says that over the country, one in six of the homes on which their members lend is pre-1919. In Scotland the figure is nearly one in three.

Among the societies approached on this subject, the Abbey National say they have no reluctance to lending on older properties. 'We take them fairly freely, with no restrictions whatsoever. The only limiting factor is the amount of money we have available.' With an insurance guarantee policy they will lend up to 95 per cent on such a property: in fact they accept 75 per cent of the loan with an insurance guarantee of 20 per cent. The Nationwide say much the same—that they will lend up to 75 per cent of valuation with no strings attached. With an insurance guarantee they will go up to 85 per cent.

A medium-sized society, the Lambeth, while charging one-quarter per cent more on properties built before 1930, will lend up to 95 per cent of valuation, if topped up with the guarantee. 'On sound older properties, not too large, we are prepared to lend on the same basis as on other types,' they say.

If for some reason you have no luck with building societies, you can try banks or finance companies. Borrowing this way could be more expensive and for a much shorter term. And if you can't get anywhere on your own you might see if a mortgage broker could help. But remember, anyone can set up in this business, so choose a well-established firm if you can, and get a clear understanding from the outset on whether you will be charged for their services, and at what rate, and if there is to be a charge for abortive work if they also fail to get you a loan.

Do read carefully anything you are asked to sign. Better still, ask your solicitor to look it over and get any arrangement clearly in writing. The Corporation of Mortgage Brokers, 6a The Forbury, Reading, Berks. is a small group which is trying to improve the brokers' image and whose members have established a code of conduct for themselves. They can put people in touch with members in different parts of the country.

An insurance broker might also be able to help—many loans are tied to insurance. The Corporation of Insurance Brokers, 15 St Helen's Place, London EC3, and the Association of Insurance Brokers, Craven House, 121 Kingsway, London WC2, can supply names. Another possibility is a private loan. The person selling might be willing to 'leave something on the property'. Or your solicitor might be in touch with possible sources.

If you are buying something old, see if you are eligible for any improvement grants. Your council offices or Citizens' Advice Bureau can give you leaflets about these. You may be able to get up to half the cost of modernisation (including professional fees) to a total of £1,000. This means that you have to find or get a loan for the other £1,000, or part of it, yourself. But you do not have to pay back the grant, nor are there any restrictions. You may let or sell afterwards if you wish.

Discuss the work with the local council before you start. They will tell you the procedure for making an official application with estimates and plans. And you must make sure you have the right approval notice before you begin. If you are having other work done it is easy to get confused with forms, but approval for building regulations or planning purposes is not the same as grant approval.

The grants are available through your council and come in three forms—standard, discretionary and special. The first two are the ones likely to be of use to a person improving a second home.

Standard grants are made to help meet the cost of providing a fixed bath or shower in a bathroom; a wash basin and sink; hot and cold water at bath, shower, basin, or sink; and a lavatory. If you had all five improvements you could get up to £200 or more if you had to build on a bathroom or install cesspit or septic tank drainage, or bring piped water into the house. To qualify for this type of grant the house must have been built before 3 October 1961.

Discretionary grants are more elastic and subject to a

Page 35 Two converted barns: *(above)* this one has perhaps lost its character but has become very homely; *(below)* tithe barn, now a stately home

Page 36 More conversions: *(above left)* watermill—last used as such in 1928: *(above right)* oasthouse-original staircase retained but windows in kiln roof no longer permitted by Kent authorities; *(below left)* folly, now a miniature house; *(below right)* once a pub, the sort of property that could make a holiday home

total of £1,000 for each house improved, or for each dwelling provided by a conversion. But where flats are made through conversion of a property of three or more storeys, the top limit of grant is £1,200 for each flat. Different councils seem to have different ideas about discretionary grants and what sort of work is eligible. So again it is probably better to have a chat first with someone who handles these, if you can, before you start form-filling. Cost of work must be at least £100 before this grant will be given.

Grants are paid when work is finished, though discretionary grants may be given in instalments. Some councils keep a list of builders who specialise in this sort of improvement work.

If you choose a builder who is a member of the National Federation of Building Trades Employers you should be able to get a loan of from £150 to £750 towards the amount you have to find yourself, through Forward Trust, a hire purchase subsidiary of the Midland Bank.

As the result of an agreement between the two, package deals can be arranged which provide the loan, obtain any necessary planning approval and ensure compliance with building regulations.

Interest is $9\frac{1}{2}$ per cent for up to five-year loans and 10 per cent for those up to ten years, with life cover included.

If the old property you plan to improve is in a development or intermediate area you can get still higher grants for modernising—up to 75 per cent instead of 50 per cent of the cost, or £1,500 instead of £1,000. But the work must be completed before June 23, 1973.

The areas to which these extra benefits apply are principally in the North, East Midlands and Westcountry. They take in parts of such popular holiday home districts as Northumberland, Yorkshire, the Lakeland counties, Devon and Cornwall. So check whether a property you have been con-

c

sidering comes into a higher grant section of the country. If there were a choice in different areas it might influence your decision.

It is possible if you buy a very old place, that it may be 'listed', which means it has been recorded as being of special architectural or historic interest. All buildings built before 1700, which survive in anything like their original condition are listed and so are most buildings built between 1700 and 1840.

The point about this is that under the Local Authorities (Historic Buildings) Act, 1962, authorities are permitted to make grants or loans towards the repair or maintenance of such properties—as distinct from improvement grants. Some authorities do, and some don't. But it is worth quoting the Act to them (or even buying a copy and waving it under their noses) and seeing what they will do. And if you are really going to get enmeshed in fighting authority over an old property, Cambridgeshire & Isle of Ely County Council's *A Guide to Historic Buildings Law* (50p) sets out the essence of legislation on the subject in layman's language.

Having considered how you may be able to get money for your second home, it is necessary to point out one way in which you may have to be prepared to lose some.

When you own two properties capital gains tax rears its ugly head, and if the time comes when you sell your second place and make a profit, you may have to hand some over to the taxman.

For 1970/71 and subsequent years you can be taxed up to the rate of 30 per cent on the gain on a property other than a principal private residence unless, during the year when you sell, the total proceeds of all your disposals of capital assets do not exceed £500 or, for 1970/71 but not for subsequent years, your total gains do not exceed £50.

38

If you bought the property before 6 April 1965 and sell
at a profit you can assume an even rise in value from the
date of purchase to the time of sale, and start measuring
the profit for tax purposes from the April 1965 date. Or you
may elect to have your chargeable gain determined by
reference to the market value of the asset on 6 April 1965,
instead of by the time apportionment.

A husband and wife living together still count at the moment as one for the assessment of tax, so nothing is gained
at present from that angle by having the second property
in the other's name. From 1972/73 they can elect to be
taxed separately but in any case that applies only to earn-
ings. You can, however, claim exemption for a second home
occupied rent free by a dependent relative, but only for one
such home.

Solicitors' and estate agents' fees on sale, cost of advertising the property for sale and similar expenses can be set
against the gain. So keep a list. It it also possible to set
against the gain the cost of certain work necessary to bring
the property into an inhabitable state.

Suppose that in 1966 you bought a country cottage which
was not a main residence and not therefore excluded from
capital gains tax. It needed a good deal of money spent on
it. The drains were defective and part of the roof needed
retiling; you spent £600 on having these dilapidations
made good. In 1970 you had the cottage rewired at a cost of
£120, and the outside painted for £100. In 1971 you added
a further room, costing £450. And in 1975 you sell the
cottage.

Against the price obtained you would be entitled to set,
in addition to the incidental costs of acquiring it, and disposing of it, the £600 for making good dilapidations at the
time it was taken over, and the £450 for the additional
room, (provided, in the former case, the effect of making

good the dilapidations was still evident—in other words, that it had not been allowed to fall back into disrepair). But the cost of rewiring and repainting would not be allowable against a capital gain as they would be regarded as normal expenses of maintenance, although they could be allowable for Schedule A if the property was let.

If the district in which the cottage was situated was deteriorating and you sold for a loss, the same rules would apply. If you sold for £1,000 less than you gave for the property, that £1,000 and the amount of the other allowable expenses would be available to set against any other capital gains you made in the same year, or in the future. But you could not set it against your other income.

Incidentally the last twelve months of occupation does not count, as that is allowed as a changeover period (ie, in the course of simply buying one house and selling another you might find yourself for a period with the two on your hands).

All this, of course, is only a simplified version of what the taxman has to say on the subject. There are the usual ifs and buts, depending on your circumstances, and it might be worth getting an accountant to see if he can track down any loopholes to your advantage.

CHAPTER 4

Where to look

Where to look for a leisure home will for many people depend on where you live.

If you want a place for weekending it will have to be reasonably accessible. Country areas around big cities and coastal regions within reach of them are the most popular for this sort of use. But if you are thinking mainly in terms of holidays, then your recreational interests can play a larger part in the choice. Will you want sailing, swimming, walking, bird-watching ... and in a group, or in escapist isolation? Can you afford a reasonable price or must you limit yourself to the least expensive possibilities? Will it be only for yourself and family, or do you hope to let? If the latter you will have to think of other people's possible requirements as well as your own.

In Britain the most popular holiday areas are Devon and Cornwall, the Lake District, the south coast, Wales and Scotland. Naturally it is in these that many people have acquired holiday homes, and here letting is probably easiest.

But many getaway homes are found in East Anglia, comparatively near to the crowded south-east and with its supply of often moderately priced cottages. You should look in and around off-the-beaten-track villages in Suffolk and Norfolk for these. From the other side of London families go to Thames-side retreats, or perhaps to a timber home on an island in the river (bought for a price the original owner would never have dreamed of). They may go further, into Dorset or Wiltshire, or, like many Midlanders, tear off to Wales on a Friday evening. Compared with other regions Wales has a high proportion of second homes.

From Cheshire and Lancashire escapists head for the Lake District, to cottages with stone walls $2\frac{1}{2}$ft thick, or to converted boathouses. Yorkshire businessmen make for the Dales and their own coast. Fugitives from Newcastle drive across to Hexham or further still, to the more remote Northumberland villages; others prefer the salt air of the coast. The Cotswolds take Birmingham weekenders, for whom the M5 makes it an easy trip, and this area, like the New Forest, attracts people who buy the more expensive properties intending to retire to them later.

The motorways are making it possible for us to go much longer distances in a reasonable time and so they widen the areas of choice from many cities. Thus while the Westcountry is at present too far for the majority who would like a leisure home there, it is possible that by about 1980 the number of people within three-and-a-half hours' drive of Dartmoor National Park will have more than trebled as a result of motorway building. New road bridges over water previously spanned only by ferry services (eg, the Tamar, Severn and Forth) produce a similar effect. The weekend-home prospects arising from Channel tunnelling could be endless of course.

You will pay most to be by the water, in an area of scenic beauty, a green belt or conservation area. But you may think it worthwhile, particularly if you plan to retire there.

If you want a holiday home in some of Britain's finest scenery look in one of the ten national parks—Dartmoor, Exmoor, Brecon Beacons, the Pembrokeshire Coast, Snowdonia, the Peak District, the Lake District, the Yorkshire Dales, the North York Moors or Northumberland. There is nothing to stop you buying property in these districts, but planning regulations are tighter if you want to alter or extend. You have to keep close to local requirements: a pitched roof and local stone or roughcast finish in the Lake District; granite and slate and horizontal rather than vertical lines in Snowdonia; gable-ended roofs, doors and windows set deep into the walls, and garages incorporated into the main house in the Yorkshire Dales.

If you want to build, the same applies. You are unlikely to get permission to put up anything in the open countryside, but you might get a plot in a village or hamlet. Some of the park authorities produce helpful booklets on building or converting in their areas. Addresses of all the authorities are obtainable from the Countryside Commission (which watches over national parks), 1 Cambridge Gate, Regents Park, London NW1.

Should your main requirement be something inexpensive just as a base for holidays and from which you can make daily excursions, look in the less attractive former mining areas of inland Cornwall—after all, in no part of the county are you more than a brief drive from the sea. Or find a terrace cottage in a Welsh village. It may have a grey slate roof rather than thatch, and lack honeysuckle climbing up the wall, but it could be within easy reach of water or national park. And though everyone wants his cottage detached, one in a terrace could be warmer and less likely to suffer in the absence of its owner. Being right on the coast is fine when you are there, but that can be a hazard if you are a part-time owner and there are storms or floods.

43

Lincolnshire, like Norfolk, is a low-price county. You just might get a fen cottage there for £700, but anything below the £1,500 mark will probably have outside sanitation, no bathroom, and be no sort of proposition for the do-it-yourselfer whose sole previous experience has been putting up shelves and making coffee tables.

Cottages are the main choice for weekend and holiday homes on the Isle of Wight. You can reach the island in ten minutes by hovercraft, or three-quarters of an hour by car ferry ('as long as you book your passage in January for June', commented one resident). Nothing is exactly given away. You can pay £3,000-£4,000 and spend another £1,500 on it. Or there are bungalows in plenty from just over £4,000, say the agents. Flats are also bought for use in the summer months. An area like Seaview, a village on the outskirts of Ryde, is half empty in winter for this reason.

Forget the Channel Islands. They don't encourage non-resident purchasers these days. Outsiders might only get a chance to buy the most expensive property and even then permission would have to be obtained. 'Anywhere where this doesn't apply, there is nothing to buy', said one of the agents handling island property. Neither do the Scillies welcome holiday-home buyers who leave a ghost-town atmosphere in winter.

A place that often seems to get missed in such searches is the Isle of Man, although it has fine scenery, a minimum of traffic and is only thirty-five minutes by air from Liverpool. If you are thinking in terms of eventual retirement, its taxes are lower than in the UK and by arranging your finances correctly you might be able to take advantage of this. The Isle of Man Tourist Office, Douglas, will give details.

The surest way to find a bargain in the Republic of Ireland—if there are any left—is to go over and scout around. But if you can't spare that much time, get the names of Irish agents from the *Estates Gazette,* or from the Irish Tourist Office, 150 New Bond Street, London W1. Get the Irish papers—the *Irish Times, Irish Press, Irish Independent.* You can buy them from their offices in the Fleet Street area of London and some English newsagents stock them. Find out which day of the week each carries most property advertisements, and place an order for that day's edition.

There are certain restrictions on buying in Ireland. Non-Irish cannot have more than five acres unless they get permission from the Land Commission in Dublin. There is nothing sinister about this; it is really an agricultural restriction and the result of an application to buy more would depend on where the land was and the purpose for which it was being bought.

The Republic is divided into tourist regions and the regional tourism managers have lists of places that holiday-makers can rent, so if you get a property there and want to let it you could ask for it to be added to the appropriate list. The Tourist Office in London would give you the address of the manager for the area in which your property came.

Building costs are high and labourers scarce (they have all come to England) so prices are not low for anything new. For old property, they seem to vary a good deal. Around £2,500 was said to be a cheapest in the Galway area, and the same price was quoted for an improved cottage with an acre in Limerick. Water was from a pump. 'But', said the agent coyly, 'you don't need to mention about that.' A Sligo firm said you might get a cottage in the country for £2,000—though they hadn't got any. There certainly wasn't much joy for the woman who wrote to a Cork agent,

45

asking for a cottage 'up to £500, with at least ten acres'. Mind you, they can at times produce something at that sort of price—without the land and minus one or two other odds and ends like a roof!

But if you are thinking of Ireland you can get generous grants for improving a property. On a three-room house you can have up to a third of the cost of work (up to £100) from the state and a similar sum from the local authority. The grant goes up to £120 from each for a four-room house, and to £140 for a five-room property. So if work costs £420 on a house that will have five rooms when improved, you have only to find £140 yourself. Nor is that all. You can get £50 from the state and the same amount from the local authority towards bringing in water, and £25 from each towards sewerage. If there is more than one dwelling within the house, grants will be available for each.

Don't start work until you have been in touch with the authorities. Details about grants can be had from the Secretary, Department of Local Government (Housing Grants Section), O'Connell Bridge House, Dublin 2. Then when you have your cottage all jollied up you can try letting it to nostalgic Americans for £35 a week.

When you want to use it yourself, there are many routes and permutations of routes to Ireland. You can fly from Heathrow, London, and from Manchester, Liverpool, Glasgow, Leeds, Bradford, Cardiff, Bristol, Birmingham, Edinburgh, Blackpool, Castle Donington, Newcastle, Southampton and Exeter, to Dublin, Cork, Shannon or Belfast.

Ireland has a selection of car-hire services and most of the major companies have representatives at the airports. The Irish Tourist Office will give you names of firms. If you prefer to take your own transport, British Rail, the B & I Line, the Belfast Steamship Company and others operate car and passenger services. By one of these you could go from Liverpool to Dublin, Swansea to Cork, Holyhead or Heysham to Dun Laoghaire, Fishguard to Rosslare, Stranraer to Larne, and Heysham, Ardossan or Preston to Belfast. There is also a motorail service from London to Rosslare, via Fishguard.

In Wales the holiday caravan ranks high among leisure homes, letting being done by the owners or by site operators. Porthcawl is said to have the largest holiday caravan site in Europe. There are also cheap bungalows, chalets, holiday flats and modernised cottages, which estate agents handle. In Tenby three firms have 600 such properties on their books, which they let for owners from about £20 to £50 a week in summer.

The main letting season is from the spring Bank holiday to mid-September, but is lengthening. Letting is quite an important consideration for most owners as it covers rates, which are high in areas with a small permanent population and a big influx of visitors. Many owners, in fact, live some distance away and may use the properties for three or four weeks and some weekends—or not at all.

One firm found that flats let best, for about twenty-two weeks a year if by the sea. Inland they might let for sixteen to eighteen weeks. You could get up to £30 a week in the high season, they said, for a two-bedroom flat sleeping six; in spring and autumn, about £17 a week. 'Put in good beds and furnish in a homely style—not rubbish, but things people are not afraid to sit on. We find people are honest about damage. If they break anything they report it. One broke a Woolworth tumbler worth 9p and left 25p to pay for it.'

At the height of the season there might be only three hours' turnover between one tenant leaving and the next

47

arriving, so it was impossible to have all the places cleaned by charwomen. Outgoing tenants had to be relied on to do this. But the firm did make a cross-section check.

Pembrokeshire was probably the most popular letting area in Wales—perhaps in the whole country, according to another agent. And there was winter letting here too, with industrial development bringing in non-residents.

The sort of thing that interested the buyer who wanted to use his holiday home as an investment was a scheme of flats, selling at about £3,400 each, to include carpets, cooker and refrigerator. Furnishings would come to £200. Rates would be about £50 and repairs and decorations another £50 a year. Management charges would be about 10 per cent of amount obtained. But the owner could expect £400 a year or more, plus his own holiday.

You might get a derelict cottage, said this agent, and do it up with grants so that it cost about £3,000 modernised—but anything suitable was hard to find. A bungalow at

Holiday home in Canebières

£4,000 was a better investment if it was in the right situation, with money coming in immediately and no repairs to think about. Or there were chalets in holiday parks, from about £2,750. The value of holiday properties could rise quickly in the right location. 'We sold one for £2,650 and resold it the next year for £1,000 more.'

It is sometimes possible to get a plot for £1,500 in a seaside area, but there is a big demand for anything that comes up.

Apart from straightforward holiday-chalet parks, recent leisure developments in Wales have included a mixed harbourside project in Caernarvonshire. The properties, termed boating lodges, are modern cottages, flats and maisonettes, designed to have a casual waterfront look, of differing heights and with outside staircases leading to sundecks. They were priced from £3,545 to £5,750.

In Merionethshire a former army camp has been turned into a holiday village with Norwegian log cabins selling

Trybo chalet in Norwegian surroundings, but equally at home anywhere else

from £2,200. You lease the plot for thirty-five years at a ground rent of £60 a year, plus rates. The arrangement is that after this you can renew the lease, take the cabin away, or sell it to the site owner. The intention is to have 350 cabins, also a clubhouse, swimming pool, tennis courts, dance hall, shops and a restaurant.

In Scotland, Perthshire and Argyllshire are the areas to which Glasgow executives and their families go to recoup—or perhaps down to Kircudbrightshire or Wigtownshire. The west coast and sea lochs attract some, and all are on the lookout for cheap shells of cottages they can do up, the one requirement being a view. Not many bargains are likely to be found within this sort of distance of city life. Although in the remote north you might still get something for £300 or £400—with spring water and a mile walk to a car road.

Looking for a Scottish weekend or holiday property from a distance is not easy unless you have personal contacts, perhaps made through previous holidays there. House buying and selling is handled rather differently in Scotland. A good deal is sold through solicitors as well as through agents and you will probably be asked to make an offer under a tender system, the highest bidder getting the property.

The small type of place you might be looking for could be on a private estate. Landowners offload some of these at times and you might see them advertised in Scottish newspapers and in the more serious national papers. You could try putting an advertisement for what you want in one or two Scottish papers like the *Campeltown Courier* or the *Ross-shire Journal* and see if anything turns up. *Willings Press Guide*, which should be in your public library, will tell you what newspapers circulate in any region. The National Trust for Scotland, 5 Charlotte Square, Edinburgh 2, might have something you could rent.

If you do organise a Scottish holiday home and want it to earn you rent in your absence, tell the Scottish Tourist Board, 2 Rutland Place, Edinburgh 1, and the Highlands and Islands Development Board, Inverness—who cover seven counties. Both keep lists of places available for letting and will be glad to put yours on them. 'As long as it doesn't actually look at the gasworks, there should be no difficulty in letting a holiday property in the summer in Scotland for many years to come', was the verdict of the Tourist Board.

If you live in London or the south, remember the cost of getting to and from Scotland. In terms of time, however, by air plus car-hire, or by motorail, many parts are surprisingly accessible compared with, say, south-west England or farthest Wales.

CHAPTER 5

Cottages (of course)

What should you choose for your holiday home? Almost anything might do if it was in the right situation. Most people go for something easily run. Beyond that it is just what suits them.

A small family would presumably seek something compact—no one wants extra work in a leisure place. They would probably look for a small garden that wasn't much of a headache either. But other families, with lots of youngsters, or who planned to let, might prefer a property that slept as many as possible and a large garden where children and dogs could run wild. And if you are letting it is sometimes useful to have a spare room in which to lock away special possessions.

So while most people will want a cottage, bungalow, chalet or holiday flat, others may be on the watch for something cheap, but good value; or amusing; or full of character. The rambling old vicarage, the rundown mill, the folly, the redundant station, tower or lighthouse can all find buyers among second-home seekers. Yet another type of family, who simply want to save the bother of travelling to

Page 53   Today and tomorrow: *(above)* a far cry from the caravan from which it is descended: a Bluebird Caravans 'Penthouse' with angled bay window, two bedrooms, lounge, kitchen and bathroom; *(below)* a leisure home of the seventies shown by Waterside Plastics in 1970

Page 54 Canadian style but equally suitable the world over: *(above)* a factory-built A-frame cabin is made in several sizes by different manufacturers: the exposed cedar decking is attractive and combines low maintenance costs with excellent insulation—Fisons Construction; *(below)* wide decks of Western Red Cedar provide living space for this uneven site and are very durable—design by Christopher Pulsy, West Vancouver

the sea at weekends, will settle for an ordinary house on an estate—if it is near the beach.

Cottages are the most discussed of the various types of holiday homes, partly because they seem to have a special sort of meaning to the Englishman. It is his dream to have a welcoming hidden-away cottage home, with thatch and roses and clematis. And then, for years people were able to pick them up cheaply and some made good money improving and reselling. Capital gains tax rather spoilt the market for the semi-amateurs in this field, although the more generous improvement grants are bringing back a few. There is also something of a status rating in owning a cottage. Another point is that they are often in village or hillside settings which are more appealing than the less individual surroundings of mass produced modern small homes.

A cottage is somehow a more personal thing than a bungalow or a holiday flat. For one woman the suggestion that she might let her cottage when she was in town seemed almost sacrilege. But a lot of this cottage aura is wishful thinking. Today, a really cheap cottage may have an interior soaked with rain from a collapsed roof; it will be dark, with small rooms and windows, and brown paint; floors, roof timbers and window frames will have rotted. Water will be from a pump, or at best a cold tap in the kitchen. What passes for sanitation will be outside. Its rural seclusion will probably be largely due to shoulder-high brambles filling the garden, or to the fact that it is surrounded by fast roads or motorways. Mention this sort of place to the average building society and they will turn green.

Even so, agents do manage to sell even the most derelict cottages, though usually for cash; often a buyer just wants the site, if it happens to be a good one. It may represent his only way of getting a weekend place in that spot of pro-

55

tected countryside. The better-sited cottages are frequently auctioned, no matter what their state, and they can draw a lot of bidders. Agents invariably suggest taking them to the saleroom if they get a batch at one time—if, for example, a landowner is consolidating his estate or if a farmer goes in for more mechanisation and, needing fewer agricultural workers, has their cottages for disposal.

Sussex agents recently auctioned a group of these and so many hundreds of people turned up that many intending bidders could not get into the hall; one woman burst into tears when she got the cottage she had been battling for with a rival bidder; and a man, not getting the place he wanted, simply bid for another cottage he had never seen and was quite happy when he got that, knowing he could not lose on it.

Later when the same agents had a further collection of estate cottages for auction they had 2,000 requests for particulars and from all parts of the world, including India. This time they put up a marquee in the owner's ground for the sale, and eleven workers' cottages fetched £85,300, all going to private buyers.

If your choice of cottage is going to be something with four walls and a roof, or perhaps no roof, and you are going to start almost from scratch in restoring it, remember that if you spend too much you may find it hard to get your money back should you need to sell. This is particularly true if you add expensive touches to suit your own taste when a more run-of-the-mill version of the same thing would suit another person just as well. If there are similar properties dotted around, try and find out what is the top price they sell for when on the market. If you would need to sell yours for much more to cover your projected outgoings, you had better seek ways of pruning your expenditure. Converted cottages do fetch high prices, but there is a limit at which intending buyers dig in their heels.

It depends, too, on how well you do your improving. There are two kinds of cottage restorer: the botchers who spoil the feeling of the place, putting in picture windows, flush doors, pink mirror glass and generally reducing the appeal, and their own chances of a good price. The others are those with a flair for seeing the possibilities that many people would miss; who do a thoughtful job, changing as little of the original as possible and taking pains, when they make alterations, to match not only window frames, bricks and roof tiles, but smaller details like door latches.

If you are not going to engage an architect for your cottage improvement, but just a local builder, you may feel you need to get someone with an experienced eye to supervise what he is doing. And unless you know a good deal about the subject—or the builder—this would be advisable. After all, anyone can set up in the trade. A chartered surveyor who specialises in building will do this for you. You can get names of building surveyors from the Yellow Pages in the telephone book, or the Royal Institution of Chartered Surveyors, 12 Great George Street, London SW1 will tell you of some in your vicinity. But the main High Street estate agents usually have a building surveyor on the staff and you could ask him to do the supervision. The fee would probably be negotiated on the basis of time involved.

If a property is 'listed' you will not be allowed to alter its outside appearance much, as least in the front, and will have to get permission for any work which might affect this. However, don't turn down a very old property because of this. You sometimes see quite major extensions being made to such buildings. Like everything else different authorities use their powers to different extents, and one area may permit what another would not.

If a cottage proves to have rot or woodworm there is no

need to be frightened right off. But it is better to get a specialist firm to deal with this rather than a jobbing builder who may not be drastic enough in his treatment and so lay the foundations for an even bigger bill in a few years' time.

There are hundreds of timber-treatment firms, many of whom also give a twenty-year guarantee. (This in fact only relates to the wood actually treated and can be of little value if the firm ceases to exist.) They give free estimates and you should get two or three, as these vary. Some firms have their own work teams and an estimate will cover the whole job. Others will only be quoting for treatment and there will be the additional charge for a building firm to take up flooring, replace affected wood and so forth. The British Wood Preserving Association, 62 Oxford Street, London W1, will send a list of members (whose work will have been investigated) and information on different processes.

If you can afford to put in some form of central heating while the other work is being done you won't regret it. Damp is one of the worst enemies of old properties, especially of the second-home variety that may be unused for long periods. You are likely to use such a place more, and beyond the summer months, if it can quickly be warmed up. Many people with holiday cottages like to spend Christmas in them.

You can get advice about the most suitable and economical heating system from the National Heating Centre, 34 Mortimer Street, London W1. They take into account things like frequency of use, situation of the property, whether there would be room for an oil tank and if it would be easy to get fuel delivered. They will also supply a list of firms on their register, who operate their two-year guarantee scheme. (They make a small charge when it comes to giving detailed advice.)

If you are thinking not in terms of restoration but of a cheap property just for weekends, you may decide not to bother about a survey. You may plan to rebuild most of it anyway. Even so, there is no need to take on something with a serious problem that could make it hard to sell if you want to get rid of it later, or that would be continually costing you money to keep it habitable.

If you are determined to be your own surveyor, and have some practical knowledge, you may find *Guide to Domestic Building Surveys* by J. T. Bower (The Architectural Press, £2.50) of assistance.

A property that seems damp may be harbouring wet or dry rot and the latter could land you with a great deal of expense, for once in a building it can spread all over. Affected wood and plaster will have to be taken out and renewed, and surrounding areas treated, and you won't know until the work is well under way just what size bill you will have to face.

So look carefully for possible causes of dampness, examine the extent of the damage already done, and try to assess how much it will cost to put right.

Very tightly fitting floorboards, without the usual sixteenth of an inch gap between them, and a ring of rust round the nails are signs worth noting. They could indicate condensation beneath the floor, causing the boards to swell —a happy hunting ground for the dry rot fungus.

If you watch a surveyor at work you will probably see him doing some toe-to-heel rocking in the centre of floors. This is to test for any suspicious springiness. If the ends of joists are rotten, floors have a spongy feel. Should it come to the point of getting floorboards up to see what things are like underneath, take up about three beside an external wall, where there is most likely to be dampness. A strong torch and a hand mirror will increase your range of viewing.

Note the situation of chimneys and where there should be fireplaces even if they have been filled in. Blocked un-ventilated disused flues can produce condensation. Gaps in the mortar of brick or stonework are more obvious sources of dampness. Creepers may look attractive on the wall, but could be hiding or causing trouble of this kind, and the roots of trees close to the house could be responsible for damage to foundations or drains. The root system of pop-lars, for instance, is very extensive, and willows can form masses of root fibres in drains and completely choke them.

Check for blocked gutters, especially in valleys of the roof, and for cracked or broken water and waste pipes. The backs of downpipes can be a source of trouble; they often rust, if they cannot be reached for painting, and let water into a wall. And look out for white stains on walls at the sides of pipes, where water may have overflowed from a blockage over a considerable period. Moss on the wall at the bottom may be another pointer.

Blocked air vents, and thick foliage growing round such vents can be causing dampness under floors. Broken or missing roof tiles are obvious things to look for. With some kinds of tile brighter red patches are a clue to the fact that they are flaking. You can get a better view of these and of gutters if there is a dormer window to lean out of. Faulty flashings round chimneys can be letting in rain.

Moisture can be introduced by earth in flowerbeds bridg-ing the damp course. Where dampness results from lack of such a course, or deterioration of one, there are various ways by which these can be inserted. Firms who deal with woodworm and dry rot often do this sort of work as well.

Close-fitting linoleum over unventilated or imperfectly ventilated wooden floors can be another cause of dampness leading to rot: bathrooms and kitchens often suffer through this. Sections of new wood in floors, panelling or skirting that do not quite match the rest, need to be explained. Why did the replacement have to be made? Signs that should leave no doubt about the presence of dry rot are a layer of reddish-brown dustlike spores on floor and ledges; a musty mushroomy smell; rippling lines on wood going along the grain; or worse, cracks against the grain, when decay is more advanced. Flaking paint may have several causes, but one could be rot, so inspect carefully.

If an owner admits that there has been dry rot but says it has been dealt with, go into exactly what was done and make sure the trouble has not started up again.

When badly decayed wood is taken out it should be burned and at least two feet of the good cut away beyond the affected area in all directions, to allow a safety margin. Plaster that has housed the fungus must also be cut out, for at least a foot round and beyond the area of trouble. Walls should be thoroughly sterilised, and treated timber used to replace the rotted wood. Naturally the original cause of the trouble must be identified and put right.

Even a simple building like a cottage can have dozens of different forms. Most attractive, when restored, are the timber-frame Tudor ones, perhaps with a projecting upper storey to give stability to the floor, and the traditional exposed interior beams and inglenook fireplace. These are best-sellers on every agent's list and seldom cheap if in a reasonable state of preservation. Since, like antiques, they have a rarity value they are generally a good investment.

You get a whole range of regional cottage types. One of the oldest has cob walls—a mixture of clay, gravel and straw—and you find it in the Westcountry. But you are less likely to find a lending source on this sort of property. In the same area you get solid-looking granite block cottages, and these don't lend themselves to much prettying up. You also get the fishermen's cottages, similar to their counterparts in Scotland, with a stone outside staircase to the upper floor and a lower floor that was generally a store. Originally they may have been whitewashed, and modern colour-washes and imagination can do a lot for these, especially as they are often in interesting settings round harbours or off cobbled lanes.

In the south-east you can get weatherboarding, long timber slats stretching across the building. These may be painted white in Kent, or tarred in Essex. Norfolk traditional clay-lump construction sounds offputting but is simply another form of cob. It may be topped with pantiles. In Suffolk exterior cottage walls may be plastered and tinted pink or some light shade. In Kent, Sussex and Surrey they may be hung with tiles, either plain or ornamental, to protect the timber frame. A more matter-of-fact version of this idea is the slatehanging used in the Westcountry.

In Wales you will get stone and slate; in more rural parts of Scotland the single storey 'but and ben' (outer and inner room) place, probably of stone with a rush-thatched roof.

You get flint cottages on the chalk ridge from Norfolk to Dorset and carefully detailed limestone ones in the Cotswolds. Westmorland produces its own stone homes, sturdy with low pitched roofs and protective porches to withstand a rougher climate. There are bonnet-hipped roofs in Huntingdonshire and elaborate black-and-white exteriors in the west Midlands. In some districts you will find herringbone pattern brickwork filling in timber framing, and everywhere the more recent and less popular Victorian cottages, some over-ornate, others featureless.

If your dream cottage has to have a thatched roof there

are plenty in existence—probably 60,000 in Britain. But thatch can vary from shaggy-looking straw, like a pony's mane, to trim fresh Norfolk reed, twelve inches thick and crisp as a new broom.

Most thatch is found in Norfolk, Suffolk and Essex, but you get it in Dorset, Wiltshire, Hampshire, Devon and Cornwall and other areas, though generally south of a line from the Wash to the Bristol Channel. The types you are likely to find are long straw, combed wheat reed and Norfolk reed (which is the longest lasting and can have a life of sixty years). The latter is the type that is taking over as replacements are made, since this reed is being grown specially for the work while other types of thatching material are disappearing in the wake of the combine harvester and modern methods of agriculture.

A thatched roof provides excellent insulation, with thermal properties equal to a boarded and tiled roof and a one-inch thickness of glass fibre. There is no reason, moreover, why rethatching a cottage should cost much more than an ordinary roof. But price does depend on how far the material has to be brought. And once it has been done, it is wise to have the roof inspected every two or three years. The ridge, especially, must be kept in a reasonably good condition.

Undoubtedly there are drawbacks. One is that you must first catch your thatcher. Although there are over 600 in the country and more are being trained each year by the Council for Small Industries in Rural Areas, 35 Camp Road, Wimbledon Common, London SW19, the work is slow and if you are going to need a thatcher you should book him six to nine months in advance. Another drawback is that building societies won't rush to lend on thatched property. But insurance is the thing that makes people hesitate.

One man told me about his H-shaped house in Essex, the two parallel sections of which were tiled and the middle section thatched. The thatch had deteriorated and he had it taken off; the quote for rethatching was £500. In fact he had this section tiled, but as the work cost £400 and the tiles £96, there was really nothing in it pricewise. But— the insurance premium came down by £30 a year.

Actually, say CoSIRA, you rarely hear of thatch catching fire, and there is an intumescent paint that can be used on the timbers and injected into the thatch which, in the event of fire, expands and sets up a barrier, excluding air and preventing the trouble from developing.

Fire insurance rates differ, so try several companies. The Country Gentlemen's Association Insurance Brokers, 54 Regent Street, London W1, quote rates for thatched property, in a satisfactory condition, of about 40p per cent on the building and 50p per cent on contents, compared with perhaps 9p per cent on brick and tile and 20p to 25p per cent on contents. CoSIRA can suggest other sources for good insurance rates and they can put you in touch with master thatchers' associations in England. The Small Industries Council for Rural Areas, 27 Walker Street, Edinburgh can give addresses for Scotland.

Thatch addicts might also be interested in CoSIRA's book *The Thatcher's Craft*, £4.20.

The same organisation has lists of firms producing handmade bricks, wrought-iron work, ceramic tiles and other products that could be useful if you are restoring an old property. But often you needn't look farther than a village builder for old materials. They are wise to the demand for the stuff these days and store what they don't need. And they generally know where demolition work is going on. The Yellow Pages will give you names of demolition firms, who may have their own stores of salvaged bricks and tiles.

Another source of bits and pieces for use in renovation work is The Cottage Men, Buckland Wharf, nr Aylesbury, Bucks. They often have old oak beams, pantiles, second-hand bricks, antique ironmongery and such things for sale. They are cottage restorers, with improved cottages for sale, and they do a certain amount of cottage agency work.

I know the purists will shudder, but Reamcrest, 241 Main Road, Sidcup, Kent, produce extremely realistic reproduction oak beams and wall panels—with 'grain, knots and adze marks'.

If a property you are restoring needs reroofing, Redland Tiles, Redland House, Reigate, Surrey, have a reroofing loan plan through which, if you use their concrete tiles and their approved contractors, you can borrow up to the total cost of the repairs. Loan arrangements are made in conjunction with the United Dominions Trust.

If you have to replace a staircase, a spiral one might save space. Or you might want to match windows, or see what can be had in floor tiling. You can collect ideas and relevant literature at the Building Centre, 26 Store Street, London WC1, or at building centres in many of the bigger cities.

A great deal has been written on converting cottages. Two other books that might interest anyone setting out on the trail are the popular *Your Country Cottage—A Guide to Purchase and Restoration*, by Robert Edmunds (David & Charles, £1.75), and *Converting a Cottage*, by Suzanne Beedell (Sphere, 37½p). The *Homefinder* magazine's book department, 199 Strand, London WC2, stock a range of inexpensive titles on property buying, surveys, building regulations, financing, house plans and so on. They will send a list on request.

A garden with a holiday cottage can be a boon or a bore. It depends how you feel about gardening and where you live the rest of the time. Even if some land is part of the attraction, you don't want to have to tackle a jungle every time you visit the place. And the simplest things can spell work. Grass needs regular mowing during summer and gravel paths have to be weeded. With a country hideaway you may arrive each weekend to find that rabbits, squirrels and sometimes deer have been pruning on their own account.

So don't be too ambitious. If you have any real acreage with your cottage, turn it into paddock and arrange with a farmer or riding school to put a horse to graze there, or you may find someone with a donkey that will perform a similar service. If it is only a small garden, the easiest way of keeping it neat is to pave the area and add interest with tubs of conifers or bulbs. Heather, tidied up once a year, goes on blooming for ages, and shrubs are no trouble. Alternatively, opt for cover plants. *Ground Cover Plants*, by Margery Fish (David & Charles, £1.75) and *Plants for Ground Cover*, by Graham Stuart Thomas (Dent, £3), will guide you.

There is no magic formula for finding the ideal, or indeed any, cottage. You try agents (the weekly *Estates Gazette* gives the names of estate agents all over the country, broken down into counties and towns), comb local and national papers, enquire in pubs and shops in areas that interest you. Find out the names of local farmers and approach them, and landowners and ring their estate offices. Read cards in newsagents' windows. You can try writing to the owners of properties that catch your eye, in case they might be intending to sell: I know of one man who wrote to seventy owners before he clinched a deal with one of them.

There are central sources you could contact. The Forestry Commission, 25 Saville Row, London W1, sells off a few of its cottages from time to time. Often they are in a poor state and people buy them just for the site. But sometimes they 'actually have windows and doors', as they put it. Those for sale are usually offered by tender. At times they also lease cottages. Either way their twelve conservancies would know if anything was available in its own area, and their addresses can be got from the Commission.

The National Trust, 42 Queen Anne's Gate, London SW1, does not sell properties but sometimes lets them on, say, twenty-one year leases. Often the arrangement is that if a tenant will carry out modernisation the rent will be comparatively nominal. Here, too, head office can give addresses of regional offices from which local information is available.

Coastguard cottages surplus to requirements are disposed of by the Department of the Environment, Marsham Street, London SW1. They can give you the location of the regional office you would have to contact, or you could find these from the phone book—there are offices in the main provincial cities.

The British Waterways Board, Melbury House, Melbury Terrace, London NW1, sometimes have canal cottages vacant. They also have a vast waiting list. They advise people to have no illusions. Anything unoccupied is probably the subject of a demolition order, or completely lacking in services, or is a mile up the tow path, or would cost the earth to make habitable. And the local authority wouldn't give much encouragement in that direction either. Just to complete the picture—such places have probably been inspected by hundreds of dedicated cottage seekers already and turned down even by them.

Everyone thinks it would be wonderful to get a 'but and ben' in the Highlands for practically nothing, but it is not quite as simple as that, points out Oban architect Bill Crerar, whose firm gets the job of sorting out some pretty primitive ones in this part of the country and on the islands.

Even so, he does make it all sound rather simple and admits that people who spend £2,000 on a £2,500 cottage—helped with improvement grants—can often sell later for £6,000 or £7,000. But you will certainly have to pay £2,500 for something in a good situation, needing improvement. You might get away with £1,000 in a poor setting.

Thinking in terms, say, of the type of cottage the Forestry Commission sells off—one that has been lived in, but needs a lot of work to make it comfortable—Bill Crerar says water will usually be available although you may have to pipe it in. Or if you can get water within a reasonable distance but have to put in a storage tank and pump, the cost need not be excessive. Allow £25 for the pump.

A septic tank might have to be put in, costing between £150 and £200, depending on distance and type of ground. A modern fibre glass one might be cheaper. Either way it must be at least 60ft from the house.

Electricity is not usually a problem as the Highlands are well served with this. You might have to bring it 300 or 400 yards at a cost, say, of £100 per 100 yards. If you do have to have a generator this could be £350, but you can often get a secondhand one; you find them advertised in local papers in areas where mains supply is being brought in. Electricity boards can tell you of such areas.

Running costs for a generator will not be heavy, but you won't get much heating from them. And even if you only expect to use your cottage in summer it is still advisable to have some form of heating—it could need drying out after being unoccupied during a long wet spell.

Night storage heaters seem to be the best bet, but make sure the floor will hold their weight. Joyce Lowrie goes into the subject of heating such cottages in detail in the *House & Gardens Book of Cottages*, Collins & Condé Nast, £4.25. (But see also page 58.)

CHAPTER 6

Oasthouses, lighthouses, boathouses

Bakeries, butteries, barns and boathouses; coachhouses and chapels; follies and forges; inns and police stations—even a county jail; oasthouses and mills (wind and water) by the dozen; schools, stations, stables... Suggest what you like and someone will have converted it.

One family in Cornwall teamed up a cowshed with a pigsty and cottage to make an oriental style three-part home and guest section. It looked nice with its thick stone walls and hillside setting, and needless to say, the finished product did not have the appearance of a cowshed and pigsty.

I spent every weekend one summer going over a selection of such conversions. It had to be weekends because this was the only time many of the owners were there and they were all so proud of what they had achieved that they wanted to be around to explain how they had got over this or that problem. And indeed they had done very well, although often the original point of picking up something cheap to make into a weekend home got lost in their enthusiasm for turning ideas into fact.

If such a miscellaneous collection had anything in common it was attractive siting—on hilltops and watersides and in spots where you would never now get consent to build anything new. But there was another common factor and this was the pleasure the owners had found in refashioning their properties.

There was curry lunch one Sunday with a watermill family, with the constant diversion of the river rushing beneath the mill and visible through a window slanting out over the water. You came to accept the roar of the waterfall, and away from the mill everything seemed strangely quiet and lifeless.

Two friends had bought the large ungainly building with its wheel, and split it into four homes. But mills are not an easy conversion; a lot of precautions have to be taken against damp when you live over water. Here damp courses were put in and the walls lined with insulating blocks. There was old machinery to move, and holes for pulleys and belts to deal with. The height of watermills—this one was 45ft—can make them far from cosy and often there are adjoining buildings which can hardly be left empty. Here there were heavy beams which came in strange places when rooms were formed—though they added to the character if you did not mind ducking occasionally. And the solid walls, as in all such buildings, tested ingenuity in the disguising of piping and wiring.

But the proximity of moving water gives opportunities for effects with floodlighting, and for streams and waterfalls through the garden. It also has to be watched carefully at times of heavy rain.

Then there was tea with the windmill people, who had five floors and seventy-eight stairs to go up and down. They put vacuum cleaners on three floors to save the carrying.

The mill walls were 18in thick and sloped inwards. A slight snag from the owners' point of view was that they

Page 71 Norwegian Log Co house built in Scotland: *(above)* the walls are of logs and the roof covered with grass and heather; *(below)* the very simple construction can be seen in this interior view

Page 72 *(above)* This interior of a Cedarworth timber house shows how comfortably informal wood can be; *(below)* this prototype holiday house has a protected dining area beyond the low-level terrace—designed by Hird & Brooks, Penarth, and manufactured by William Cowlin & Son, Cardiff

could not have a fireplace and they found the rooms lacked a focal point. But a general drawback with windmills is that as they are naturally in very exposed situations they get the worst of bad weather.

Another windmill owner had made four floors in her weekend home: an ultra-modern kitchen, bathroom and dining area at ground level; an 18ft-diameter living room on the first floor, centrally heated and with some of the original machinery forming the ceiling. A spiral staircase led up to a bedroom and cloakroom and another staircase to the second bedroom. In this mill the actual top floor housed water tanks; in the other it had been made into a small sitting area, with views in all directions.

The owner of the second mill had had to spend a lot of money 'ridding it of creepycrawlies'. But she enjoyed the 'divinely beautiful views' as she lay in her 15ft circular bedroom 'way, way up, like one's own private Hilton'.

John Vince's *Discovering Windmills* (22½p) and *Discovering Watermills* (25p), both Shire Publications, provide much useful information. Incidentally the same publishers have in their list *This Old House* by David Iredale (23p) which might be of interest to anyone owning an old property and, as most owners are, curious about previous ownerships. The author gives guidance in tracing the history of an old building.

Mills come on the market quite often, although rarely at low prices, since their situations generally attract converters. On the other hand they are liable to be quite large, and with the watermills there may be serious damp problems, so they are sure to have many more viewers than serious buyers, and they frequently go to auction.

The Society for the Protection of Ancient Buildings, 55 Great Ormond Street, London WC1, have a Wind and Watermill section that might be worth contacting by own-

E

ers of this sort of property, or by anybody seeking to become an owner. But the same society is also a useful general source of characterful and sometimes inexpensive properties. You can become a member for a yearly subscription of £2.10 and receive the lists they issue every few months of 'threatened' buildings of architectural or historic interest, for which they hope to find sympathetic owners or tenants. At times these are offered at low prices or rents, to attract people who will improve the places, or save them from demolition.

SPAG does not handle properties itself, but gives the names of owners or agents. Write to the Society (enclosing a stamped addressed foolscap envelope, for they are a voluntary body) and they will send you an old list to show you the sort of thing you would receive were you to become a member. When you do eventually become the owner of a really old building they are able to provide information on its restoration and preservation.

Here are some of the places you come across in their lists: a row of sixteenth- or seventeenth-century almshouses in Devon which 'could convert into one house of great interest', 2ft-thick walls of stone, rubble and cob, not modernised but main services available, £1,500; a 'beautiful Elizabethan brick house' in Dorset, 'now in a pitiful state but well worth saving, as are its stable block and old brew house'— price by negotiation; a chapel of ease in Wiltshire, the chancel still intact and 'the rest in ruins, but the whole quite charming and conversion to another use a possibility, keeping the ruined part as a feature'; a windmill and cottage in Essex, £5,000; a fifteenth-century timber-framed hall-house in Suffolk, divided into two cottages, 'only a sympathetic purchaser can now stay the threatened demolition'; a small country church and adjoining schoolhouse in Staffordshire 'should convert very well into a home'—between £1,000 and £1,500 asked. There was also a seven-teenth-century Cornish windmill; the gatehouse to a Wilt-shire castle—£7,000; a detached thatched cottage of stud, lath and plaster at the edge of a village 'in real country' in Cambridgeshire, needing extensive modernisation; and two former church schools in Wiltshire.

The Historic Buildings Bureau, 2 Marsham Street, London SW1, part of the Department of the Environment, also produces lists of such properties for which owners or tenants are sought. There is an estate agent in Bromley, Kent, who specialises in this sort of property and in getting loans on it, and in most areas with many old buildings you will find one or two agents who carry much more of that type on their books than the others.

A big old house in the country, to be used by various branches of a family together or separately, could prove a useful joint venture in second-home owning. An unmod-ernised farmhouse should not be expensive, out of com-muter range. The wing of a country mansion, somewhere off the beaten track—with large rooms to daunt most buyers —could be wonderful for letting children work off pent-up energy, and would probably have a garden to scale. Yet the price could be low.

Rambling old parsonage houses can sometimes be bought comparatively cheaply when they come on the market the first time, straight from use by the last incumbent and un-modernised. They have been known to have twenty or thirty rooms, but something a little less generous would probably be more suitable.

I remember a U-shaped vicarage through which one picked a path around the buckets placed to catch the rain that came through the roof. The bathwater was heated at one tip of the U and piped across an open courtyard to the

75

bathroom at the other tip. Not surprisingly it was seldom even warm. However, with the roof repaired and one arm of the U demolished, it became a comfortable, manageable and pleasant building set in a lovely garden. Anyone who bought that as a country retreat would not in the end have regretted it.

You can find out from Diocesan Dilapidations Boards if any *p*arsonage houses are coming on the market in an area. The Church Commissioners, 1 Millbank, London SW1, will give you the address of the board responsible for an area that interests you. But actual sales are handled by estate agents. Certain agents in a district tend to get church properties more than others, so if something like that would suit you, find out about the agents and keep in touch. Lots of vicarages and rectories are still sold off each year. In 1969/70 the figure was 191, and the previous year 195.

The days of the railway carriage weekend home are over. Now, if anything, you buy the whole station. Plenty have passed into private hands, although local authorities can be sticky about granting planning permission for use as homes.

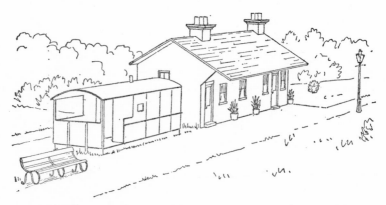

Railway halts sometimes turn into second homes

Western Region have sold off between 200 and 300 stations in the last five years—but not more than a dozen have actually become homes. That is not for want of interest. On one occasion when they were offering some for sale they had 3,500 letters of enquiry, to say nothing of the phone calls. Ugly as most of these Victorian buildings are they seem to exert a fascination over the most unlikely people, who turn out to have a longing to own one. It must be something to do with never having become an engine driver after all.

You can write to the Estates Valuer for any of the regions of British Rail and ask if anything is coming on the market —they are usually put in the hands of local estate agents, who often auction them. Being forewarned is being one up on competitors, so make a note of any intended station closures you read about and keep making specific enquiries. They usually go for quite sensible prices. The Western Region ones averaged about £2,000 to £3,000. The station for Sandringham, used by royalty, fetched £5,700 in 1968, and with it the buyers got solid oak panelling that they thought must be worth thousands.

All sorts of possibilities suggest themselves. You could make the booking hall the dining room, with the ticket office for the kitchen, and the serving hatch already there. You can have a sort of one-up-one-down (platform) home. Or you could use the platforms as terraces and put a sunken garden, or drop a swimming pool, in the gap. In theory, that is! In fact your station may have no water or drainage and could still be using oil lamps. The chances of getting planning permission for the use of this sort of property as a home would be slim, unless there is a stationmaster's house there that has already been lived in. You could promise to sink a well, bring in a generator, and build a septic tank, but they still probably wouldn't be impressed. They

77

don't encourage scattered homesteads these days. It costs too much to empty your dustbin.

I talked to one man who bought a station in the late sixties. He got a booking office, main and ladies' waiting rooms, signal box, stationmaster's house, the platforms and a little land. He had seen the station advertised and went to look at it. He found 'thousands of other people' doing the same. He could not get a mortgage, but offered £3,500 himself, and this was accepted. He was able to move into the stationmaster's house, so there was no planning problem.

He and his wife did some repainting, to get rid of the railway colour scheme and spent a little on improving things. They took in the signal box as an extra sitting room, and enjoyed having the platforms to themselves to sit out on. Among their earliest—rather surprised—visitors, were the two sons of the first stationmaster, making a sentimental pilgrimage to the old place that their father had left when he emigrated to Canada at the beginning of the century.

If you drive round Kent you will see a great many oasthouse conversions, and some agents in the county usually have a few converted or unconverted oasts for sale. But don't fall for a comparatively low priced unconverted one unless you are sure there is planning consent. Hundreds have passed through agents' hands in recent years because farmers, making better use of hops, are finding they don't need so many oasts and can sell them for healthy sums. It doesn't necessarily follow that the authorities consider their location suitable for homes. If they do agree to their use for that purpose you will find that in Kent they want to ensure that the building keeps its original character, with the cowl retained and painted white, the kiln roof-line uninterrupted by windows and the intrinsic form of the oast preserved. The Weald of Kent Preservation Society can give further guidance. (And you can buy inexpensive fibre glass cowls.)

You find oast houses in other counties—Sussex, Hampshire, Herefordshire, Worcestershire. They are mostly about a century old and you could pay £6,000 or more for one, even unconverted. Made into homes they can fetch high prices. They seem popular with businessmen who sometimes have so much work done to them that, apart from the curve of the walls of the rooms made in the kilns, there is little left to tell that the place was an oast. Some have square kilns, so even the curved walls may be absent.

Oasts can make big properties, as there may be two or three kilns, and barns and other buildings may be incorporated. But they are not the easiest of places to turn into homes. You have to damp-proof and put in floors and do a lot to the interior. Often they have been used as stores by their farmer owners. One man said, 'You could have got drunk clearing out mine—the floor was deep in fermenting, squelching, rotten apples.'

Another owner found the records of hop yields for a hundred years in the oast house he took over. A third woke up one morning to find himself covered in feathers that had blown down through a hole in the ceiling he was working on, from a bird-nesting area below the open cowl.

The Martello towers dotted round our south-east coast sometimes stir the imagination of would-be weekenders, and indeed they do come on the market. One was recently being offered by a London agent for £10,000 and it was estimated that bringing services to it would cost another £5,000. It was in an ideal second-home situation, looking on to an estuary, and had eight acres of land, a moat and a landing hard for boats. The building was 40ft high and could have been made into an interesting holiday place,

79

with two bedrooms, dining and sitting rooms, studio and roof garden.

The idea of Martello towers stems from Corsica. They were introduced to Britain for defence in Napoleonic times. Once there were over a hundred in the south-east and a few others further afield. They were built for about £2,000 or £3,000. If you have thought of looking out for one you could always ask the Ministry of Defence if they are likely to be disposing of any more—they have sold off thirty-five or more already, and only a percentage of the original number remain intact.

However, you would be wise to think well first. According to the account given me by the architect of one of London's modern landmarks, who converted such a tower for his weekend home, it is obviously not a job for amateurs.

At beach level the external walls are 13½ft thick, slimming towards the top, and the parapet is about 34ft above lower floor level. The average width of the tower is 44x40ft, making it slightly elliptical. There are enough bricks in one of these towers to build thirty or forty houses and the walls are so tough that it took two men with a compressor and two drill guns three weeks to form the bedroom wardrobes in the architect's tower.

Now the building contains a hall, dining room, kitchen, guest suite and housekeeper's flat, also the owner's bedroom suite and lounge, and above, a sun roof and tiled patio.

In a storm one year waves broke over the roof and the garden was under water. The owner went down to the lower ground floor to see if everything was all right when something broke a window. Water poured in, sending furniture swirling round the room, and was almost at ceiling level by the time the owner managed to get out.

In spite of such hazards, he said he was deeply attached to his historic second home. One of his favourite jokes is the overheard comment of a passer-by: 'Fancy anyone being daft enough to build a house like a Martello tower . . .'

This type of conversion is often done by architect owners who can see a future in the original buildings. Take the case of the stables acquired by an architect because he was attracted by the roof timbering. Indeed, he turned the building upside down, putting the bedrooms on the ground floor and the living room in what was the hayloft, so that they could 'enjoy' the roof more often, with its pattern of beams.

The stables were, in fact, L-shaped, with a single storey adjoining a double-storey part. They had taken eleven horses. The architect kept part of the ground floor for garaging; this was on one side of an arch. On the other side were three bedrooms. The floor was raised several feet to reduce unnecesary height and to provide storage space— and perhaps a mushroom-growing area. There were also bathroom and utility rooms on the ground floor.

Above, in the sitting and dining area, the rough stone was painted white and left exposed. The roof was suitably insulated and the complicated pattern of supports and columns left uncovered to create interest.

On the same level there was a kitchen, studio, cloakroom and an open terrace reached through a door in the glass wall of the sitting room. Additional windows were made, but as much of the building as possible was left in its original form to retain atmosphere and keep down expense.

This only dealt with the double-storey section. The single-height part was to be considered later—an indoor swimming pool, perhaps?

Unquestionably it is better to build up your plan as you go along if this is possible, rather than start right off with everything cut and dried. All sorts of ideas occur to you as you live in a place, ideas that wouldn't present themselves during casual visits. And you get to know draughty corners, and unexpectedly pleasant areas that catch the evening sun or prove to have interesting views. You begin to notice the spots in the house to which the family gravitate, and consider how they might be developed as sitting areas. And you find that certain complicated, costly alterations you had planned may not be necessary at all, as some simple alternative has turned up.

There is no reason why your second home should have less style than your day-to-day one. I met one woman with a small place in Chelsea who acquired a castle in Ireland as her second property. Castles in Ireland come in a whole spectrum of states of repair and sometimes at quite reasonable prices—if you are not too fussy about what you get.

This owner planned not only to make a flat for herself in part of the castle, but to do up some cottages that came with the property and let them as holiday homes.

Her description of the castle as 'in a dreadful condition' was no overstatement. 'There was a fountain of water coming through the front hall; the entire roof had to come off and had to be rebuilt. There was a sort of sewage system, but no hot water, or heating. Frogs and tadpoles came out of the taps.'

One tower was a mass of green mould and ferns and had to be gutted. The circular staircase 'came to bits'. Blocked drainpipes had flooded another part of the building. A horse with a penchant for looking at himself in the windows got inside and fell through a floor (he was retrieved from one of the cellars none the worse). The owner's dog fell through another floor in a tower—but also came to no harm.

Anyway, the owner got what grants she could, employed direct labour and when I last heard from her was getting on well with her repair programme.

A couple who bought a pub in Norfolk did so because they wanted a place with large rooms. It was auctioned and there was only one other bidder; as it was in a poor state they got it cheaply. They kept the name of the pub as their house name, and put a dovecote on the post on which the sign had swung. Occasionally people have been found inside, looking for the bar, thinking it is still licensed.

They had to scrub nicotine off the ceiling in one bar— there had been three—and they pulled down some of the many partitions and took away doors, which seemed to be everywhere. They made the drawing room out of the biggest bar, made a new kitchen to replace the outhouse one, and another area became the dining room. One of the upstairs rooms became a bathroom, the others remained as bedrooms. The large cellar proved useful for many purposes besides housing the central heating boiler.

The owner certainly got the place for a give-away price (by present standards) when he bought it—this was a few years ago now. But admits to having spent seven or eight times the amount he gave on bringing the place up to scratch. Even so, pubs or inns are worth looking for. Breweries cutting out their less profitable establishments— often the more out-of-the-way ones and most suitable for weekend places—sometimes put them on the market at a price that takes into account their need for modernisation.

One man I met had made his second home out of a Wesleyan chapel he bought for £250 in 1963. The chapel was 20x30ft—the same size as the flat of one of his architect friends, so this friend was asked to redesign the chapel on similar lines to the flat. It was in good condition, with solid stone walls and a slate roof, and in its heyday it had held 100 people. It stood on a gusty corner of moorland, on the curve of a road, with nothing to obstruct its view in any direction.

The main alteration was the insertion of another floor to make two storeys in the building. There was still space after this for a loft above. The new floor was partly supported on steel poles, now painted white and doing service as room dividers. A staircase was put in, also a picture window in a previously blank wall, and dormer windows. Three bedrooms, a bathroom and lavatory were made in the upper floor. Downstairs was designed on open-plan lines—with a dining and sitting area and a kitchen, separated by room dividers.

Ends of pews were incorporated in panelling round some of the rooms. Two bible cupboards were put to more general use, and a type of lectern helped to do dividing duty downstairs. The tall narrow white-framed windows with their pointed arches were not altered, but louvred shutters, the same colour as the front door, were added to brighten the building.

'The chapel did not have to be de-consecrated, but we had to undertake not to brew alcohol here, or engage in games of chance—which was very reasonable', said the owner. It was his plan to use the chapel for holidays and when he retired, in ten years or so, to live there permanently with his wife. With the purchase of a little extra land for a garage he thought his total expenditure had amounted to about £5,500 and he was well pleased with the result.

A large number of such properties have been sold by the Methodist church since 1931, when they became redundant after the amalgamation of Wesleyan Methodist, Primitive Church and United Methodists. Others are still coming on the market from time to time. They are sold through estate agents, but if you want to find out if anything is likely to be coming up in a particular area contact the minister of the circuit which covers it. The church authorities say they have found such properties in 'the more delectable areas' like Devon, Cornwall and the Yorkshire dales' much sought after as homes.

You won't get much joy out of ringing up Trinity House and asking if they have a spare lighthouse—though some have been sold over the years, when a change in the sea or sands has reduced a tower's usefulness. These are sometimes offered for resale.

The owners of a Yorkshire lighthouse loved it. A particular attraction for them was that from the living area with its semi-circular stairway, they could go up a ladder to the lamp room and surrounding balcony and watch superb sunsets over the water.

Barns, like coach houses, are old friends in the conversion world. They offer plenty of scope and you don't have to spend a fortune clearing out inner floors, partitions or machinery before you begin.

One family I knew had divided their barn, making one section a double-height sitting room, and putting four bedrooms and a bathroom in the other. They made use of an adjoining cowshed for kitchen, dining area, utility room and garage. The addition of a damp course and central heating made a lot of difference to their comfort.

Another barn had a wonderful wagon-roof, which the owner made the feature of the place when it became a home, siting the dining and sitting rooms in this area. Previous conversion work had been done at some time to the building and there was a gallery with a priest hole, and a viewing window from the gallery down into the dining room. The gallery is now reached through a wardrobe in the main bedroom, which everyone finds rather amusing. The building now has three bedrooms, two bathrooms, a kitchen and study as well as the two large feature rooms and, like many barn conversions, looks more attractive inside than out.

One weekend when the whole of Kent seemed to be flooded I remember making a hazardous journey across the country to visit a family who had made a folly into a part-time home. The building was in fact so damp that the central heating they had installed had to be kept on, winter and summer. But when I visited it, in spite of the weather outside, the place was extremely comfortable.

Follies come in all sorts of guises, and people love them for odd weekend places. If they show signs of being popular they usually go to auction. One in Somerset—a 120ft tower with 120 steps to the top, set in a disused cemetery, caught the popular interest and the agents had forty or fifty people making serious enquiries about it even before they had announced the date of the sale. Again much of the attraction was the situation, with its fine views. Coastguard and lock-keepers' buildings, and more smugglers' hideaways than ever there were smugglers, also attract buyers because they are near a waterside and have uncluttered views.

Small village schools are frequently converted into homes, and are worth considering for holiday places as they can often be bought quite cheaply. This is because, unconverted, they do not look too inviting. They are tough buildings, and show it, with few concessions to prettiness. The interiors are just as uninspiring and you can almost smell the hot milk and gym shoes as you go round.

It needs a lot of imagination to do much with these buildings, often squat and Victorian looking, in stone, brick or flint, and surrounded by a grey playground. But this is another type of property on which you won't have to spend much money and time in ripping things out at the start. If it is single-storey you may find space to build another floor, or a half-floor, which you can partition to suit your needs. If you feel like altering windows and entrance doors, that might help; and tearing up the tarmac play area and putting some sort of garden round the building will make it more homelike.

A great many schools have been changing hands recently, as the authorities have been regrouping for economy. Between 1966 and 1970 1,375 primary schools and 791 independent schools were closed in England and Wales. Some of these in villages will certainly have gone into domestic use.

I remember a property called 'Boys and Girls' coming on to the market, and people asking the agents the origin of the name. In fact it had been a school, and the owners had taken the name boards from the separate entrances, joined them and used them as their house name. This calls to mind another conversion with an equally puzzling name: The Fox with its Teeth Drawn. This had been an inn called The Fox, but the new owner, a teetotaller, decided to make it quite clear that the property was no longer used for its old purpose though it still kept its old name.

CHAPTER 7

'Big boxes' and holiday parks

'Holiday homes' in the many parks that have grown up round the country to take them, are a comparatively inexpensive way of getting a change of scene.

These 'homes' are what the caravan trade know as 'big boxes' or 'holiday statics', one of the many types of accommodation descended from the affair you tow behind the car, which the trade calls a 'tourer' and you probably call a caravan. The only actually mobile descendant is the motor caravan, which is car and caravan combined.

The 'holiday home' or 'static' is a large caravan, not intended for towing, but designed simply for leisure use as a sleeping place and centre for families who would normally be spending their days out of doors. Much more sophisticated and intended for permanent living, is the residential caravan, also known as a 'mobile home'—which only adds to the confusion, for it is anything but mobile in the normal sense of the word. This has a sitting room, kitchen, bathroom and one or two bedrooms. Beds, wardrobes, floor coverings and curtains are included in the purchase price, which may be from £1,000 to £3,000. A more spacious

88

version, the twin unit (really two together) usually has three bedrooms and can cost from about £2,000 to £3,000.

The 'big boxes' have wheels and towing bar—but these are only to make moving it round the factory or site easier. They are taken to the park on a low-loader, and once on the hard stand are jacked and blocked up and may not move again.

There are about 202,000 static holiday caravans in this country. They have fewer divisions and 'trimmings' than the residential versions. There may be one bedroom and a lavatory, and the rest is sitting room/kitchen area, well equipped with seats that turn into beds (the dining table may do so as well) so that six or seven people could sleep in the unit. Prices go from about £600 to £1,200.

Bluebird, a subsidiary of Caravans International which is the largest group of caravan manufacturers in the UK, produce a range of these and also of residential units with their greater accent on comfort, which they find people buy for weekend retreats and also for retirement homes. Their Penthouse model, 30ft long, architect designed and selling at about £1,258, would, they say, be very suitable for an inexpensive weekend 'cottage'.

Other well-known makers of both tourers and statics are Lissett, Pemberton, Belmont, Omar, Donnington, Fairview and Willerby. The International Caravan and Camping Exhibition at Earl's Court each November is the place to go to if you want to make comparisons.

The caravan world is well served with magazines which you can study—*Caravan, Modern Caravan, Practical Caravan* and *Mobile Home* among them. David and Charles publish *Caravan Touring*, a substantial book on the subject, and *The Motor Caravan*. The National Caravan Council, 40 Piccadilly, London W1, the representative body for the caravan industry, produces publications such as *Caravan*

89

F

Holidays. Should you want to hire a static holiday caravan, they can supply a list of sources. If you prefer to buy your static, the principal manufacturers and distributors advertise in the caravan magazines. Hire-purchase can usually be arranged.

You must have a site available, to which such a holiday home can be delivered. Generally this will be in a holiday park, where occupation will be allowed for perhaps only three-quarters of the year. A residential caravan will probably go to a special park authorised for permanent occupation. Some distributors run their own parks and can let you have lists of these, or of those run by operators. Some caravan organisations, the magazine *Modern Caravan*, the AA and RAC also produce lists, and others can be bought from booksellers.

Parks may be beside beaches, rivers or mountains; on clifftops or farms; in the grounds of a manor or castle. You can take your choice of being beside an English lake, a Scottish loch or an Irish lough. You can 'sleep and play to the murmur of Atlantic breakers', or 'listen to the nightingales in our woodland park'. Or you can have the more everyday sounds of people and pop, although operators emphasise that holiday parks are quieter places than holiday camps. Some parks take hundreds of units, others, half a dozen. As a rule the big holiday parks are on the coast, in popular tourist areas. The smaller ones are inland where there is some scenic attraction.

There are about 5,000 caravan and residential home parks, licensed by local authorities, throughout the country. Here conditions should at least be adequate, with basics such as ablution blocks. But people who have stayed at a number of such parks say they can be anything from first class to—when they seem to have slipped through supervisory nets—distinctly grotty. Parks approved by major cara-

90

van associations have to keep a uniformly high standard.

Site charges may be from £35 to £75 or more a year. Usually sites are leased or rented. In the latter case you could have to move at short notice, so make sure you understand the position clearly when you move in. As one owner of a static said, 'It can be a bit of a jungle.'

If you buy this type of holiday home from a distributor or manufacturer you will probably have to pay for its delivery to site and a small fee for connection to services if these are available. If you buy a secondhand one already sited you save this. You may also have to pay rates, but these are more likely to be included in the rental.

If you want to let, or sub-let, and this is allowed by the park, you can advertise in papers like *Daltons Weekly*, the *London Weekly Advertiser*, or the caravan and camping magazines. The site operator may be willing to handle lettings for you for a fee. You might get £7-£18 a week, or more—according to season and site—for a 4-6 berth unit. Against this you will have to set site rent, cleaning and equipping, and letting fee if you do not handle this yourself. Remember to insure the unit, particularly if you are letting, (premium) £3 to £6 a year. But a lot of these expenses can be claimed against tax, so keep detailed records. And don't forget to claim your expenses for visiting the site to see all is well.

Choosing the right site will make a lot of difference to letting. Look for a popular one where things are well run and people come back time and again. Go for a unit that will stand up to hard wear—seven or eight years of it. If you only use it yourself and look after it properly, it could last twice as long. When you let, take an inventory of equipment and leave a copy where tenants can see it. Put in enough equipment for the maximum number the place will sleep. And don't try, whether you are letting or using the 'holiday home' yourself, to pack in more than the number for which it was designed—on a wet day this could lead to frayed tempers.

Mr John Bunn, with over 2,000 static holiday homes on his three parks at Selsey, Sussex, is the operator with the largest number in England; other large-scale operators are the Leisure and Gailey Groups. According to Mr Bunn, the most popular holiday statics are still in the £800 range but over the last ten years there has been a trend towards the use of the large residential version for holidays and weekends, and a desire for greater comfort in holiday parks. During the same time parks have been developing on the lines of holiday camps, but with self-catering. The best have swimming pools, restaurants, ballrooms, shops and even private beaches. The difference between the parks and camps is the greater space in the former and the more peaceful atmosphere.

A decade ago, he said, few static caravans exceeded 22ft in length and most in parks were less than 20ft. But units up to 26ft were now popular, and up to 30ft were not unusual. Some operators indeed were developing and re-developing sites with 40ft pitches in mind, with all main services to every unit. This put up site charges but many people were willing to pay to have the extra comfort.

He felt that the residential caravan bought for about £1,500 was a much more viable holiday proposition than a house or bungalow on which there were rates. He charged a site fee of £75 to £108, which included rates, and gave yearly licenses.

At a site at Bablock Hythe, eleven miles from Oxford, 99 year leases are granted, with ground rent from £110 a year. Here, by the end of 1972, they expect to have 463 holiday and mobile homes, on 27 acres with a mile frontage to the river. Generally buyers pay from £1,600 for units, which includes delivery and site connection, and furniture. In fact, with a range of eight units, most people chose one costing £1,977. The units are set in crescents linked by a road that runs parallel with the river, and the rest of the site is grass, poplars and bushes. Ducks waddle round and boats bob at their moorings (3p per foot of boat per week). There is fishing, a pub that serves meals, and a shop.

In many holiday parks and villages you will find other types of accommodation not directly descended from the caravan in that they are not movable. These are a broad range of simple buildings variously described as chalets, holiday bungalows, bungalettes, sun cottages, villas, mini-villas and holiday flats and flatlets. What they all have in common is that they are simple cheaply built units with their own cooking, washing and lavatory facilities. They may be of timber,brick, aluminium or block construction, detached, paired or in short terraces. Usually they are grouped to allow wide spreads of communal recreation space. Sometimes, if terraced, they have small blinker walls jutting out to give a little privacy.

Local authorities that are against caravan parks because they can look tatty if there is a collection of different colours and types of van, or because they feel that the number of caravan parks has reached saturation point, may give more encouragement to chalet schemes with their lower densities and more uniform look. They can bring in more rates, too. Site operators are anxious to keep on good terms with the authorities and will, for their part, go to considerable trouble to landscape parks and keep them looking trim.

If you are thinking of buying one of these chalets the sensible thing would be to spend a few weeks at holiday parks first, and try out different versions. One manufacturer said his highest sales were at the end of the year when people who had stayed in a chalet decided to buy.

Sites for chalets are dearer to rent than those for the caravan type of holiday home with communal washing arrangements, for the operator has to equip each site with water and drainage. On the other hand, because of their better amenities, chalets should get a higher rent and have a longer season. Also depreciation should be slower.

Colt bungalow

The National Federation of Site Operators publishes an official guide *Caravan and Chalet Sites*. This is available from booksellers and is a good starting point from which would-be buyers can find operators with chalets to sell. Probably not such a great many holiday home owners buy solely for investment, though a number do a certain amount of letting to offset expenses. But don't be too optimistic about possible profit. The brochures will suggest attractive probable letting figures but getting them is another matter.

Take the example of a short row of holiday bungalows in landscaped surroundings that sold from £1,975 to £2,400 leasehold. Buyers were promised £220 a year from letting. Two years later several bungalows had been sold back to the operators, who named their own price, and another was available through an estate agent at an asking price of £1,640. Net income for the first year had, in fact, been £150 and for the year after, under £100, as cost of repairs and redecoration of site had been deducted.

It may be safer to buy in parks where an income pattern has been established. But even this can be altered if more sites open up in the neighbourhood, or if there was a wet summer the year before.

A chalet building firm, who sell in bulk or individually, and who have been in the business for nearly thirty years is King's Summer Homes, 140 Streatham Hill, London SW2. They have their own parks in Dorset, Sussex and Norfolk, with letting agencies, and they claim that their chalet owners have had incomes of over £400 a year from rents. The parks are open from March to October, and on the Norfolk Broads chalets may also be occupied at weekends from November to February and over Christmas.

A chalet on their Broads park costs £1,495 and can be bought over seven years. Minimum deposit is £145. The lease is for 29 years with a ground rent of £75 a year. Legal costs are around £8. Tax relief can be claimed. Using their scheme, furnishing costs £215. Owners are responsible for maintenance and redecoration, or this can be carried out by site staff. Rates are about £22 a year.

The advantage of these summer homes over caravans, say King's, lies in the separate toilet facilities and the length of leases. 'With a caravan you normally get a twelve-monthly agreement—then a site owner can turn you off.'

The chalets are cedarwood, with 3in cavity walls lined with insulated plasterboard. Kept in good order with preservatives, they should last thirty years or more, say the firm.

95

They are mostly semi-detached and arranged round paddocks, about twelve in a group and eighteen or nineteen to an acre. All are built on concrete raft foundations, with a damp course. The owner need supply only a cooker, crockery, cutlery, pillows, blankets and a few minor items: £350 should cover the entire furnishing and equipping for six. Actually, for the benefit of statisticians, this firm finds that its summer homes are occupied on average by 4.5 persons a week.

Another large firm in the chalet and holiday village business is Larters Estates, King Street, Winterton-on-Sea, Great Yarmouth, Norfolk. They have villages in Norfolk and North Wales and sites for over 2,000 chalets which are to be built in the next few years. Swimming pools, clubs, restaurants, bars, amusement arcades, games rooms, shops and laundrettes are incorporated in the parks.

Growth in the trade has been enormous, they say. In 1962 they sold 20 holiday bungalows. At present the figure is 200 a year and they plan to step it up to 400. In Norfolk their prices start at £1,390 and they find that most people buy for investment. Their chalets can be furnished for £290.

Buyers who do not want to handle letting themselves can do it through a holiday agency who charge 15 per cent of takings. Cleaning and servicing can be sub-contracted for about 75p a week. A chalet supervisor will collect rents for $1\frac{3}{4}$ per cent. Hiring and laundering of linen for six costs £1.25 a week.

The firm offer a choice of brick and timber chalets, prefabricated in their works, with one or two bedrooms, shower or bathroom, kitchen and living room. Mortgages can be had up to nine years on up to 75 per cent of the total price (which can include furnishings bought through them). Current interest rate is 10 per cent but this varies. The minimum deposit is £250. Their chalets can be let from £12.50 to £32.50 a week over fifteen to sixteen weeks in the year, or perhaps longer.

North Wales has the longest letting season, with occupation permitted from 1 March to 31 December, and bookings are high because accommodation is short. The firm say an investor can get a gross income of approaching £500 a year from a chalet in North Wales, as against £430-£440 in Norfolk. Expenses have, of course, to be deducted from this— though when it came to decoration most people 'popped down for the odd weekend and did the painting themselves'. But owners did not spend much time in their chalets, except for the few who bought entirely for their own use.

A few estate agents specialise in holiday property. One firm in Exeter, Devon, have a dozen sites in the south-west and Wales on which they are offering chalets, usually 400-500 sq ft, from about £1,500 to £2,500. The value should go up as much as with a residential property if the lease is long enough, they say. A £1,500 chalet might fetch £1,800 a couple of years later. The owner got his holiday free, and ought to get 10 to 15 per cent back, depending on how well he let, how much he asked, the location, and how well he had bought.

According to this firm, if a chalet brings a poor return it is in many cases because of bad site management. But a lot of chalet estates have been springing up in the last year or two and they need some time to get established. An estate should expect 20 per cent rebookings each year. Another cause of poor return could be bad advertising or a bad brochure. Holidaymakers who receive a duplicated sheet from one estate and a glossy brochure from another will normally go for the latter, even if it means paying an extra pound or so. Then of course, some areas are better known than others and many holidaymakers play safe and choose the well-known resort. But there is a tendency for holiday tenants to want to get away from crowds. 'The city business-man would prefer to stay in the middle of Dartmoor—with h and c, of course.'

On all sites where these agents offer holiday chalets there is a letting agency run by the manager or owner. Usually the owners of chalets share the combined income from lettings on a cooperative basis, after paying expenses and letting fees. This works out better than each owner getting an income from his chalet only, as a manager might be induced to let one property more than another, or he might take a dislike to an owner and avoid letting his chalet.

Although the schemes offered by different site operators may appear similar they vary a good deal in detail. It is worth comparing the literature of a number before making any decisions. One may offer aluminium chalets from £1,850, furnished, on 99 year leases, at a yearly ground rent of £60; another will have chalets of reformite stone and breeze block, from £2,000, furnished, on 96 year leases, at £60 a year. A third, cedarwood, furnished, from £1,350 on 50 year leases, at £50 a year.

Mortgage rates and systems of buying differ as well. In one project loans can be repaid over five years at 1 per cent over bank rate, flat. In another, finance can be arranged over ten years at $12\frac{1}{2}$ per cent on a reducing capital. In a further scheme the loan rate is $14\frac{1}{2}$ per cent. One company offers four possible buying arrangements on the same park, including a system in which five people (not necessarily knowing each other) can join in purchasing and each will only have to put down £100 deposit.

For people who would never consider a holiday home in a large scheme, there are occasionally possibilities in smaller, out-of-the-rut groupings. These are often advertised in magazines like *Country Life,* or in the Sunday papers. There is, for instance, a batch of 'deck houses' at a yacht marina near Chichester. These square, black-and-white single-storey buildings for yachtsmen are raised above a hard standing, with space for a boat and two cars beneath each house. There is a gear store and place for oilskins at the foot of the stairs, which go up through a central pillar. On the main floor is a living room with bar-type kitchen, and french doors to a sun-deck; double bedroom; two-bunk bedroom and bathroom. They are priced from £5,500 to £7,000, leasehold. A resident harbourmaster and caretaker is on hand to keep an eye on things, put on heating for owners and leave previously ordered food parcels for them.

CHAPTER 8

'Packages', bungalows and flats

If the last thing you could endure on your relaxed week-ends would be to have other people around, get yourself a site and the necessary permission and have one of the many types of prefabricated homes put on it. This will work out cheaper than getting involved with architects and builders and having a single traditional house built. And as most of the components will be factory made, it will also be quicker.

Such homes are timber-framed or produced by some form of building system, instead of the traditional bricks-and-mortar affairs—although some makes can still be given a brick or other solid-looking skin if you wish.

Timber-frame means just what it says—the house is built round a frame of wood, like the old Tudor houses, instead of walls of brick, block or stone carrying the weight of the roof. They are lighter, warmer and drier, and without the quantities of water that go into such things as plaster in a traditional house. They produce little condensation and as interior walls are not loadbearing, internal design can easily be altered to suit buyers' needs.

If they have much outside timber as well—and some may

have clapboarded, panelled or cedar-tiled exteriors and roofs of cedar shingles as well—they blend happily into country or woodland settings and are less obtrusive than new brick.

The Timber Trade Federation, Clareville House, Whitcomb Store Street, London WC2, will send a list of suppliers. Not all sell single buildings to private buyers, but there are enough who will to provide a good cross-section, and you can tell from the TRADA list which firms take individual orders.

When you compare prices, remember that most firms will be offering different versions of the shell and you may have to add the cost of kitchen and bathroom fittings, glazing, a heating system, foundations, fencing, connecting main services and other things, as well as the cost of land. There may also be delivery charges for bringing the 'package' to your site. In some cases a team may be sent to do the building. In others the suppliers may have a builder in the area under licence to them, or they will instruct a local one for you.

Price estimates in the literature will relate to a level site, with services at hand. Should you want your building on a steep hillside and water and electricity brought across a field, be prepared to write a larger cheque. If a local builder is going to do the construction get estimates from two or three firms first, even if they appear on the manufacturer's list of 'approved' builders.

Something really woody, with a cabin feel about it, can be got direct from Norway through the Norwegian Log Construction Company, King's Lodge, King's Lane, Cookham Dean, nr Maidenhead, Berks. Prices start around £3,000 for the complete home, excluding the cost of land.

One type available from this source are holiday chalets made in standard widths of 13ft, 16½ft and 20ft, to un-

101

limited length. They can also be L- or U-shaped. As each section is prefabricated they are simple to build and it is claimed that they can be put up in five days on a concrete floor slab, or a timber floor mounted on brick or concrete piers. Walls, roof and flooring are double boarded and well insulated as they are designed to meet severe weather conditions in Scandinavia. Doors are prehung and double-glazed windows are already fitted.

The manufacturers can also supply a range of pine furniture and fittings designed for the chalets. This comes in flat cardboard cases and each piece can be assembled quickly, the parts being fixed with wooden dowels.

A Norlog home—Peer Gynt

Also available through the Maidenhead company are Norlog homes, which have the rugged look of a woodman's cabin deep in the forest. They are made of solid timbers 5in thick, each cut from an individual log to a uniform size and shape. They are joined by a tongue and groove system which has been used for over 900 years in Norway. The natural shrinkage of the wood makes weatherproof and draughtproof joints. These buildings need no maintenance or decoration and are suitable for permanent as well as holiday homes.

They have a basic plan, but this can be arranged to suit different needs. When a buyer's requirements have been agreed upon, plans are then sent to Norway where the logs are planed, prepared and shipped to the UK. An amusing version—though the suppliers prefer to press the claims of something more conventional—is one which looks rather like a railway carriage and has a roof topped with grass and heather. This is traditional in Norway, and it merges well into the Scottish landscape where some of these have been built. You don't have to shoulder the lawnmower regularly to the roof—a slow-growing grass is used, which only needs trimming once a year. For the more conventional types, the suppliers say fire insurance works out at about 10p per cent if they have a tiled roof, 11p if felted.

Guildway, of Portsmouth Road, Guildford, Surrey, say they often sell their Forest Line, one-, two- or three-bedroom timber frame homes as holiday places. Prices go from £2,450 without land, sizes from 534sq ft. They take six to eight weeks to build, and you must allow for delivery time, depending on how busy the firm is—say three months. They have also introduced an 800sq ft design, the Hereford, selling from £3,500, to cater for the demand for a slightly bigger home in this market.

Many firms who produce these timber frame houses allow

103

buyers considerable freedom of design. W. H. Colt, Son & Co, Bethersden, near Ashford, Kent, have been building in timber for over fifty years but say that most of their houses are still planned to meet buyers' specific requirements. They start with inexpensive weekend homes that would probably not get full planning permission for permanent living, and might cost £1,500 without land.

It is cheaper per unit, they say, to build a pair of semis and let one. Some people build four like this, having them designed to fit the land available, and let all but one. Their Jubilee-cottage type forms the basis for many holiday homes although it is also suitable for full-time use.

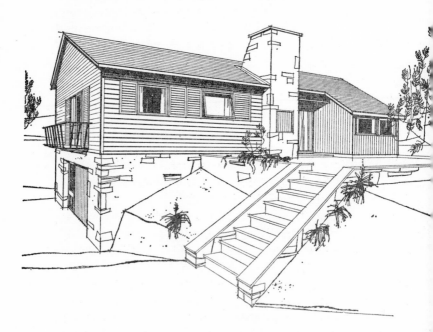

Colt Le Touquet design of holiday house, with log store that can be filled from outside, and garage with holiday tackle store beneath the house

Page 105 (opposite) These
floating homes in Chichester yacht basin have roofs
admirably suited for sun-
bathing; (below) house-
boat interiors can be snug
and warm

Page 106 These deck houses at Chichester Harbour are nearly as good as being afloat; the space below gives ample room for storing small boats

For their holiday properties they suggest the addition of shutters to secure the place when not occupied. And they advocate a plain finish—emulsion paint, simple bathroom equipment, not a lot of kitchen fittings, to reduce cost and keep below the £4,000 mark. They say the popular size is about 700sq ft.

But there is another type of demand and this is for the large holiday home, usually financed by grandparents who have a section for themselves and plenty of bedrooms for children and grandchildren. Colts get orders for these for the Scottish islands.

An inexpensive holiday home is produced by Fredericks & Pelhams, St John's Works, Tylers Green, nr Penn, Bucks. There is a choice of cladding, and the smallest size, 28 x 16ft, sells for £1,329 (cedar cladding) or £1,353 (aluminium cladding). This is without land, and delivery is extra. If two were built as a pair the cost would be £50 less for each.

These have two double bedrooms, a kitchen/living room, bathroom and lavatory. If a septic tank were necessary that would be a further £185. If electricity and water had to be brought to the site, the firm say the cost would be whatever the boards concerned charged: there would be no extras.

Such holiday homes would normally only get limited planning permission, for six to nine months' occupation a year. The firm say they have been supplying them to sites in Devon, Cornwall, Norfolk and Sussex. They can arrange mortgages up to fifteen years.

Eight designs for permanent bungalows, with the 'package' price starting at £2,088 and approximate completed price (including builder's work but not land), £4,775, are produced by Devon Lady, King Street, Honiton, Devon. They deliver the bungalow (without extra charge in England and Wales) in sectional form to the site. A builder

107

G

assembles to their drawings and connects services. Walls are 1in cladding (Canadian red cedar), 4in softwood framing, 1in mineral wool and aluminium foil-backed plasterboard. Roofs can be tiled or of cedar shingles. The firm says that some of these are in use in Scotland as fishing lodges.

They also make chalets of a different construction strictly for holiday use, which work out around £800-£900 for the prefabricated sections delivered to site. The smallest is 18 x 18ft, designed to accommodate four adults.

If you want a holiday home built very much to your own design—perhaps incorporating a studio or a children's wing, or lots of verandah space, Timber Frames (UK), Cripps Corner, nr Robertsbridge, Sussex, use a non-modular industrialised system which, they say, allows the client complete freedom to decide internal layout and external finish. Rooms can be of any shape or size, and provision can be made for extension or rearrangement. Cladding can be of brick, stone, timber, tile, rendering or various manufactured materials if they meet planning requirements.

Danish holiday homes were studied by building and civil engineering firm William Cowlin & Son, of Penarth Road, Cardiff, before they had their six types designed.

Their styles are of timber with one concrete block wall finished with textured render. The roof extends to make covered terraces on each side. The exteriors are planned not to be noticeable, but inside the natural redwood is brightened with terra cotta doors and window frames.

The emphasis is on built-in furniture, with the homes as near fully equipped as possible on purchase, so that the occupants have only to provide cutlery, bedding and food. It is aimed to give maximum space in the living areas, and compactness in the rest. Cleaning and tidying should be simple.

In the prototype design the living room has a built-in

sofa, with storage space beneath, which also serves as two beds. The dining area has a brick paved floor and robustly made dining table and benches. One bedroom has a built-in bed, with storage area below, cupboard and dressing table. The other bedroom has two bunks, bedside shelves and cupboard. It is suggested that downettes or sleeping bags can be used with the beds.

The 'bathroom' has a dished floor, with drain and threshold, so that the whole area serves as a shower tray. The timber walls are sealed to withstand water, as tiles. There is a wc, basin and shower.

The house is raised off the ground and the space beneath can be used for storing canoes and holiday gear.

The homes are designed to have a cosy, informal atmosphere and the living room has a log fireplace, as the firm feel this sort of fire provides the right sort of antidote to chilly holiday evenings.

A cooker, stainless steel sink, and folding chairs and coffee tables come with the 'package' and bamboo blinds, further tables and benches can be had if wanted.

Cowlins have their own sites on which these homes can be put—some small and intimate, some larger where there will be a caretaker. Among the first will be one for twelve fishing lodges along a river in mid Wales; another for 40 homes near the coast of south west Wales and one for 160 homes near the coast of west Wales. And they are particularly interested in developing forest sites.

Prices of the properties depend on size and delivery distance, but they go from £1,740 (235 sq ft) to £2,980 (445 sq ft) including furniture.

As an alternative to Scandinavian and Canadian timber, Scotslog, 8 Euston Place, Leamington Spa, Warwickshire, offer bungalows and chalets of treated Scottish softwoods. These can be built to their design or your own, or they will

109

supply the superstructure for you to do the job yourself. An interlocked construction is used.

The price range for a two-bedroom chalet from shell structure to the completely finished and fitted building is about £1,400/£1,500 to £2,700/£2,800. The properties, they say, are 'amenable to mortgages' and in some instances they are able to find land for siting these, particularly in North Wales.

Cedarworth Homes, Donnington, Wellington, Shropshire, produce their leisure homes in 2in-thick cedar. They studied Swedish, Austrian and US timber housing before deciding on this construction. Floors are of solid wood slabs —there are no joists or rafters—and walls, partitions and roofs are of solid cedarwood panels.

Prices go from £920 to £5,000 and can be spread over seven years. You can choose one of a wide range of designs, including an A-frame—and have it built by one of their teams, or follow their do-it-yourself kit.

Another type of system-built bungalow, sometimes used as a holiday home, is of reinforced concrete panels, and is made by Woolaways, 5/6 The Crescent, Taunton, Somerset. The rest of the bungalow is traditionally built, and the roof is tiled. Prices begin around £2,500 (excluding land, connection of services, paths and fences). They will inspect a site and put in plans to the authorities for a client. There is a £10 inspection fee, refunded if a contract is signed. Their associated company is Westholm Construction, of Ely, Cambridgeshire, who can also supply these bungalows.

Another non-timber system is that used by Kenkast Housing Division, Astley, Manchester, who also use concrete panels, and give their homes a pebble dash finish. They ask prospective buyers to think in terms of £3,000 plus land, and they will build for you anywhere in the country.

Some of the designs for North American holiday homes

are worth studying for they are more adventurous than most of ours. The Council of the Forest Industries of British Columbia, Templar House, 81 High Holborn, London WC1, can supply a brochure *Nine Vacation Cabins made with Fir Plywood* with illustrations and descriptions, and they have plans available.

Among these designs is a three-stage beach cabin. The first stage gives a deck, roof and enclosed shelter—the essentials. This is quickly built because there is very little cutting and plans are simple. The next two stages can be developed at leisure. The first is to complete the kitchen, bathroom and bunk room. Finally you build a big living room on the original sundeck and add another sundeck if you wish.

Quite different is the A-frame cabin which does, in fact, look like a capital A, or a rigid tent. The steep all-embracing roof makes a strong building. In the suggested design the kitchen, with its counter, the utility room and the bathroom are at the back, with the living area in front, looking over the sundeck. There is a sleeping balcony over the section at the back. With the two floors the cabin can sleep four to six people. Windows can be covered with wood panels when the building is not in use.

Another design has the appearance of a houseboat gone aground—they call it a twin ranch. It might be compared to a shoebox, with oversailing lid and a skeleton pitched roof in the centre. It is made up of three 16x20ft units on which are built two fir plywood 'boxes'. One contains two bedrooms and bathroom and is separated from the other, which contains the living area and kitchen by a similarly floor-sized deck.

Horizontal beams link the outer edges of the 'boxes' and above the open area between rise the rafters like a shallow tent, taking away the rectangular look; they can if you

111

wish, be covered, perhaps with a transparent roofing material.

The Council has a useful follow-on brochure also available—*Thirty-two Ideas for Building Out of Doors*—which has suggestions for designing patios, screens, an attached table and bench for outside eating, carports and other additions to a cabin home.

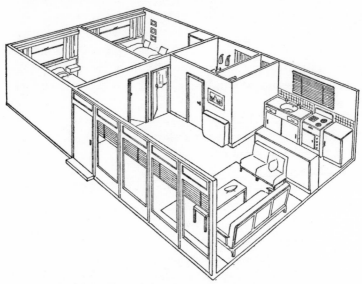

Interior of a King's Summer Home in Norfolk

When it comes to finding a site you are very much on your own.

You will of course try all the estate agents you can and you might advertise in local papers. Some people say it is better to make it plain that you are a private person and not an agent.

If you have decided on an area, talk to local people and ask if they know of anything going—the publican, postman, parson, parish councillors. A bank manager or solicitor might know of someone with a piece of garden they could be induced to sell—so might the milkman, the cleaning woman, or the gardener at one of the larger houses.

'It is surprising how it works', said a man in the prefabricated home business. 'An old lady becomes widowed. She has a fairly big garden which she cannot manage on her own and the money would be useful, so she is prepared to sell it off.'

There are a few organisations who say they are able to find sites. The Housing Enquiry Service, 415/417 Oxford Street, London W1, publishes *A Survey of Individual Building Plots throughout the Country*. It claims to list over 3,000 single plots on individual sites or small estates, from Scotland to the Westcountry. Architectural Services, 62 High Street, Caterham, Surrey, who produce house plans, will send buyers of their books lists of plots all over Britain, they also sell complete leisure buildings.

Some builders are ready to sell off a few plots on an estate if they want to get in some quick money, or if they have an oddshaped piece of land in a corner that they do not want themselves.

What you pay is up to you. A plot for one house could be £400 or £8,000 or any sum, depending on its size and whether it was, in the wilds of Connemara or on the seafront in Sussex.

If you plan to build a timberframe house you may need more space than for bricks and mortar. If it is to be clad in timber, for example, it will have to be at least 10ft from your boundary. If it is going to have a shingled roof, it must be 40ft from the boundary.

Getting a site for a second home in Scotland should not be too difficult. With the depopulation of the islands they are glad to welcome people who will build something suit-

113

able, thus giving work and perhaps letting to tourists for part of the year.

They don't encourage aluminium or static caravan-type homes. And its no good picking a site in the middle of an area of outstanding natural beauty, or in a private estate whose owner intends it to remain private. But some land-owners might be willing to sell a few acres.

You can seek your plot through estate agents, although you won't find so many north of the border, or through the solicitors who also handle land sales in Scotland (trace them through the Yellow Pages or Scottish newspaper property columns). But the best plan, says the Scottish Tourist Board, is to decide where you would like to build and go and see the planning and development officers concerned (they may be the same person). They know who owns what, which parts are available for development, what pitfalls you might come upon in that spot, and can be a general mine of advice.

The farther north you go the cheaper your land will prob-ably be—in the less popular parts you might get an acre for £100 or so. But you will need essential services, and the least expensive land will probably be the most inaccessible. So what you save on land costs you will spend on getting your property organised with electricity, water and drain-age.

You could probably get plots on many of the islands as long as they were not privately owned, or held for some special use, such as a nature conservancy.

When you have found a piece of land which you think you can buy and on which you would like to build, the question of planning permission arises.

Normally you would ensure that it already had outline planning permission for what you want to put on it. Or you would make an offer for the site subject to planning

114

permission being obtained. To buy hopefully without such permission would be to take a big risk. Of course land with planning permission is going to cost a lot more than plain agricultural land.

If no permission exists, and you decide to test your chances of building on the land an application must be made to the district council for the area in which the de sired plot is situated. To save everyone's time it is usually worth having a chat with someone in the planning office first, to see what hope there is of permission being granted.

If you then decide to go ahead (and an application doesn't cost anything) you can get the necessary forms from any district council office. They may have to be submitted in quadruplicate, so check about that. You will also have to put in a certificate stating that you either own the site or have notified the owner or tenant of your proposed application. There is a choice of forms for this, depending on your own situation. The same office will let you have whichever is applicable. You have to include simple site plans (the same number of copies as there are application forms), showing in scale the proposed building in relation to the plot, boundaries and adjacent properties.

When you have put in your application you must resign yourself to waiting—it might be six weeks, it might be months—while the authorities consult others who might be affected. If at last the application is granted, a formal planning decision notice is issued to you. If it is refused you can appeal.

If the area in which you hope to build is not zoned for housing in the first place you might as well save yourself the trouble of applying at all. But that is up to you—decisions do get altered.

If you bought the land with outline planning permission already granted, you have to follow much the same procedure to get detailed planning permission, which deals with precisely what you propose to build. You must submit similar forms, answering questions about the intended use of the land, supply of water, electricity; about drainage, access, and building materials. Accompanying plans must show design, siting, position of access and other points. All this will have to be approved before building can start. Some authorities want to have a considerable say in the look of a proposed property, others are much less concerned.

There is also the question of the building regulations with which the house must comply. Other forms must be submitted relating to what you plan to put up, so that periodic checks can be made by inspectors to see that it conforms to structural and other requirements.

Obviously you will stand the best chance of getting an application through if you get a professional—a chartered surveyor or an architect—to handle procedure and draw the plans for you. Many manufacturers of prefabricated houses will supply drawings for submission to local authorities and will handle the negotiations for a small fee.

You also have to obtain planning permission if you want to change the use of an existing building—to convert a stable into a house, for example. You have to get planning permission if you are going to divide a house into flats. But you do not have to get permission to turn, say, two cottages into one if only interior alterations are involved. Nor do you need permission to extend a house, so long as the cubic content of the original is not exceeded by more than 1,750 cu ft or one-tenth—whichever is greater—subject to a maximum of 4,000 cu ft. (Of course that applies only to one extension.) But any enlargement must not exceed the height of the original building, nor project beyond the front of it. The addition of something like a garage within the grounds of the main property is considered as part of the 'one-tenth' and does not need planning permission. But the height of such ancillary building must not exceed 12ft in the case of a ridged roof, or in any other case, 10ft, and it must satisfy the district council under the building regulations.

For this simplification of their procedure I am indebted to the Peak Park Planning Board. Different authorities have different requirements, but they will be similar to these. *Building in the Peak* (17½p), available from the Peak Park Planning Board, Aldern House, Baslow Road, Bakewell, Derbyshire, gives advice on materials, design, siting and other matters relevant to this Park.

Permanent bungalows, as distinct from the holiday chalet type, are plain sailing. Thousands have been and are being built in areas where land is not too scarce.

The word, derived from the Hindi, means 'belonging to Bengal', and this style of one-storey house was introduced to Britain by people returning from India where such homes suited the climate.

Most of our bungalows have been built since World War II (although they appeared in Kent and Norfolk at the end of the last century). Large estates have spread over coastal areas in the south, particularly around towns like Bournemouth, and also in the Isle of Wight, Norfolk and other regions popular for retirement. Some of these properties serve an apprenticeship as second homes before owners retire to them permanently.

Bungalows are not necessarily cheap, for they take more land than a two-storey property. You can get them from about £3,500 to as much as you like to pay: in the upper-price regions they become 'single-storey homes' or 'ranch houses'. Maintenance costs, however, should be lower as most of the building can be reached, and so repaired, or redecorated, by the average handy owner himself. Numerous

117

bungalow developments are regularly advertised in *Home-finder, House Buyer, Modern Home Buyer, West Country Homefinder* and other property publications.

Most estate bungalows are routine in design, usually with two or three bedrooms, and are detached or semi-detached. Occasionally there are variations such as staggered terraces or linked properties, and Spanish- or Swedish-type designs.

Flats make ideal holiday homes for people whose main object is to have a place by the sea and who are not looking for isolation or for a garden of their own. In the more expensive blocks you do get considerable privacy it is true, and generally an area of communal garden or lawn to look out on. But it is rare for tenants to make much use of this. An American once related how he stayed in such a block, and one hot summer day took a deck chair down and sat on the grass within the U-shape of the building. No one else ever did such a thing, and he awoke from a nap to find faces in all the windows looking down at him in astonishment.

In some resort areas such flats have been built in their hundreds in recent years. Generally these, too, have been built with the retired owner in mind and for year-round occupation. But many people buy them well before retiring and use them for holidays.

You pay for views of the water, but prices drop as you go back a few roads. Rates on flats, however, usually remain high.

Places like Torquay, Worthing and towns round the Kent coast are the main areas for this sort of project; but flats are also to be found in small resorts in counties like Devon. Undoubtedly they will increase in number for more and more people are wanting the comforts they offer without the upkeep of a garden. Builders like them because they make most use of costly land, and building societies are becoming more willing to lend on them.

But you need to be a little wary of buying in an area which has not previously had these purpose-built flats. What sometimes happens is that a developer puts up one block, which sells quickly but almost absorbs the potential demand. Other firms jump on the bandwagon and build more, which stick on the market. Then anyone who has bought in these blocks may have difficulty in getting his money back if he needs to sell quickly before the surplus properties have at last found buyers.

A more economical type of permanent flat would probably be something in an old house. You get big properties along Westcountry riversides that will divide into several units admirably suited for holiday use. What they lack in modern amenities they make up for in space. But buying in converted properties is not as easy as in new blocks, if you want a mortgage. Leases can be complicated if the property was not built for more than one-family ownership and resale could be difficult, so many building societies are not keen. But if you seek hard enough you will find some who will oblige. Try the Halifax, Burnley, and City of London for a start—and, of course, the local authority.

It is often possible to make a flat out of part of an old house in the country and let it to bring in some income, without reducing your own opportunities for using the house as a holiday home. The owner of a house built like a mid-European castle found that the best way of coping with this unlikely structure was to divide it into flats, using one and letting the others to holidaymakers. I know of another person who turned a nunnery into holiday flats. Some of the large white-elephant buildings that feature in the lists issued by the Society for the Protection of Ancient Buildings could provide similar scope.

The other types of flats are those built purely for holiday

use—the simplest shell, with facilities, sleeping the maximum number of bodies and only usable for a limited season. You get them in the holiday parks and in small blocks in waterside developments.

A Cornish holiday park offered a small batch for sale at £2,350 freehold (£2,610 furnished), usable for eight months of the year. They let from £12.50 to £32.50 a week, depending on season. But the park was able to offer chalets £500 cheaper, on which buyers could get rents up to £28 a week, so they did not continue with flats.

Great numbers of flats are advertised for renting in publications like *Self Catering Holidays*, from £4 to £44 a week, with one to three bedrooms and sleeping sometimes up to eight people. But where these have been built entirely for holiday use they are more often let by developers and not sold singly.

A-frame house, Canadian style

CHAPTER 9

Houseboats

Another type of second home is the houseboat—and the houseboat world is one you need to study very carefully befor you make any decisions. You can buy something coming under this heading for £200 or £20,000. You can find moorings—if you are lucky—in idyllic surroundings, on a quiet river with weeping willows, lapping water, swans drifting by ... Or you can find yourself in a houseboat colony that is virtually a slum. Moorings might cost you £100 a year or £400; you might not be able to connect with mains electricity and water. You might, again with a lot of luck get a loan to help your purchase; you are more likely to be told by most routine sources that 'we won't look at houseboats'.

Even so, there are hundreds of them dotted round Britain's waterways, yacht basins and marinas, and their easy-going atmosphere and waterside location makes them well worth considering for holiday use. One of the advantages of houseboats is that generally they need little furnishing as most of the sleeping, sitting and galley equipment is built in. You can pick up a cheap second-hand one that started life as a lighter or barge or a lifeboat by scouting round boatyards and, of course, through the grapevine of house-boat communities. You get all kinds advertised in yachting magazines.

Exchange and Mart is another source. An issue at the time of writing produces these: professional lifeboat conversion, 30ft, 3/4 berth, generator, dinghy and moorings in Surrey, £950; Thames sailing barge, converted, with telephone, electricity, engine, price by negotiation; cruiser houseboat, 30x12ft, seagoing hull, six months' free moorings, hire purchase available, Norfolk, £320 cash, or £110 deposit; 85ft converted MTB, mains electricity, water, telephone, small amount of work required, Sussex; 34ft houseboat cruiser, surveyor's report, £1,500; and an MFV needing completion of conversion work, £650, Surrey.

Occasionally you will see houseboats advertised in newspapers, or being offered by estate agents in riverside areas. Yacht brokers sometimes get them; as I write, a broker in Hampshire is seeking a buyer for a Thames sailing barge that was built in 1891. 'It probably carried 120 tons of coal', he said. 'They make comfortable places to live in, very roomy and will take a couple of sofas. Made of pickled oak. There are a number still sailing and a great many more have been converted into houseboats. This one has two double bedrooms and one single, a sitting room, dining room, kitchen, workshop'. The price was £3,250.

When it came to rating, he added, the situation differed from authority to authority. The general interpretation was that if a boat was movable under its own steam it was not normally liable for rates; but if a houseboat had been at a mooring more than three years it was ratable. Rates tend to be low anyway. The owner of a houseboat on the Basingstoke canal said she only paid about £2 a year.

If you want a newly built boat there are a few firms who produce them. Most exhibit at the Boat Show at Earl's

Page 123 *(above)* The gangplank to a houseboat can give a feeling of cutting loose from city cares; *(below)* the jet black roof and dazzling white walls of this modern cottage at Kinsale, County Cork, are also in good, marine tradition. Not cheap (£10,500 to £20,000), some of the cottages have galleries giving double-height living areas and a ski-lodge feel inside

Page 124 *(above)* This interior of a Cedarworth timber house shows how very simple furnishing can be decorative and attractive; *(below)* this chalet bungalow built by Selleck, Nicholls, Williams at St Germans, Cornwall, is obviously as suitable for retirement as for holidays

Court, London each January, and that is probably a good starting point for your search.

It is difficult to compare prices because you may be offered such different types of craft, with varying capabilities and equipment. The accent may be on the house or the boat. Some include engines in the cost; with others these may be extras; or it may just not be feasible to have an engine.

One firm makes what is in effect a mobile home on a raft, at a cost of £5,250. It has a sitting room with French windows leading on to a balcony, a single and a double bedroom also opening on to a balcony, kitchen and bathroom, and walkways on either side of the living accommodation, linking the balconies. The walls of the house part are treated marine ply, with glass-fibre insulation. The flat roof is strengthened so that it can be used as a sundeck. Beneath the 'house' are steel sub-frames and eight floats. With balconies and walkways it measures 54x14ft and it is claimed that it can safely take thirty people aboard.

Lighting and heating are by electricity and a 700 gallon water tank and 100 gallon capacity septic tank are built in. The idea is, of course, to connect to water and electricity at a mooring.

The houseboat can be transported by two lorries, one carrying the steel sub-frame sections and flotation units and the second the 'home'. The makers claim that with six people to do the lifting the houseboat can be in the water, reassembled, in four hours. The firm does not undertake to find moorings, but may be able to help clients get them on the Isle of Wight.

Moorings are one of the problems with houseboats. If you buy a second-hand one you may be able to take over the previous owner's moorings, but with a new one you will have to search for your own, unless the suppliers can help.

125

H

They are not easy to find. Most river and canal moorings are already taken up and although marinas are a growing fashion in the waterfront world, they tend to be expensive and not to want to take houseboats. Moorings might cost say 7p per ft per week or £7 or £8 per ft per year; or there might be some annual agreed payment to a yacht-basin owner.

Other types of houseboat that you can buy new include one described by its makers as an 'aqua-home'. It sleeps seven (or eleven if you have extra equipment), and the price is from £8,000, according to engine and extras. There is a 33ft Danish-made boat available in Britain, which has six berths and is capable of doing 20 knots. It costs £9,950. This, like the previous one, is of fibre glass, which reduces cost of maintenance, and this in a traditionally built boat can be quite high, since it needs regular repaintings, probably every two years, and will have to be taken out of the water for cleaning and scraping at intervals.

A trailable houseboat is offered by another firm. This doubles as a caravan when the hull is rested on a specially designed trailer, and accommodates four. It is a Canadian design, now made in Ireland, and costs from £3,795, with trailer.

Then there is one of French design, also available through British agents. It has a Boston-Whaler-type hull, is 24ft by 8ft 3in, and can be transported by road. The actual dwelling part is 14ft 10in by 6ft 7in, which the makers describe as large enough 'to house a family of waterborne meanderers'. The price is about £2,300. Yet another version of houseboat is described as a 'home from home, from sink unit to lounge settee' the 39ft hull takes household furniture. There are two styles, one sleeping five and the other seven, priced from £6,375.

Another firm produces 'flats afloat' and has an economy version, 28ft x 9ft 4in, ready to furnish, from £1,945. This has a ply hull, sheathed in glass fibre, and is aimed at the weekend retreat market. They make more elaborate models for longer stays. Incidentally this firm can rent or sell you moorings in the south of France, and will deliver your houseboat there, if you wish.

Here is a selection of firms who offer new houseboats: Windboats, Wroxham, Norfolk; F. B. Wilds Ltd, Loddon, Norfolk; Chris Craft S.A., Carl Ziegler Yacht Agency, 37 Great Cumberland Place, London W1; Comextra, 13 Flambard Road, Parkstone, Poole, Dorset; Dell Quay Sales Ltd, Itchenor Shipyard, Chichester, Sussex; Thornycroft & Tulira Marine Ltd, Kilchreest, Loughrea, County Galway, Ireland; Floating Homes, Bulls Bridge, Hayes Road, Southall, Middlesex; and Aquavilla Ltd, 45 New Bond Street, London W1.

Periodicals like *Yachting World* and *Yachting Monthly* carry advertisments for firms who will deliver houseboats to moorings. You can also track down brokers, surveyors, yacht basins and occasionally moorings from these sources.

One of the largest marinas, Chichester Yacht Basin, which takes 900 boats, has a section reserved for some 20 houseboats. They sit there like a convoy about to leave harbour, in pleasant surroundings, with views of trees in one direction, glittering blue sea in another, and a forest of masts above the moored yachts in another.

One man who had kept his houseboat there told me that the mooring fee had worked out to about £3 per foot per year, and that agreements were renewed annually. There were no additional charges for rates; electricity was 'piped' aboard and metered; water, also brought aboard, was free. Some owners cooked by bottled gas, others by electricity.

He had found that maintenance for his steel-hull boat averaged about £50 a year. It was advisable to paint it every three years, and with this there was the cost of lifting it out and putting it back in the water. Roof and woodwork needed painting every two years. He thought twenty to forty years would be a reasonable life for a purpose-built houseboat, depending on how well it was maintained and whether or not it was regularly ventilated.

Insurance is another point to remember. His worked out at about £30-£40 a year. The Navigators and General Insurance Company, 130 Fenchurch Street, London EC3, will insure selected houseboats, the rate depending on construction, size, age and where they are moored.

If the idea of keeping your houseboat in a modern marina, with all services laid on, appeals, the National Yacht Harbour Association, 31 Great Queen Street, London WC2, produce a *Yacht Harbour Guide*. You will also get a lot of useful information and addresses from *Boat World*, the Sail and Powerboat yearbook.

A houseboat has an advantage over a small house as a weekend retreat in that it is movable. Although an owner would probably not want to change moorings frequently unless his craft was more of a boat than a house, an occasional move could vary the scenery. The disadvantage is in the financing of the venture. Unless you can pay cash, or the firm or person selling can help, you may have to work hard getting the terms of purchase arranged. The makers rattle off lists of finance companies who they say will lend, but in fact most of the companies don't want to know.

The snag is that unless a houseboat can be registered it cannot qualify for a mortgage. And the Department of Trade and Industry say they don't register boats that in their marine surveyor's opinion are not navigable. So you may have to resort to the more expensive hire purchase machinery, and for this houseboats are not viewed as good risks.

'We avoid them like the plague', said one finance company. 'You get two or three sorts—the old barges built about 1898, floating round the Thames with the bottom falling out and selling for £5,000 with central heating, and as rotten as pears.

'Then there are the ex-motor torpedo boats, ex-Admiralty, built during the war, sitting on the bottom of the Thames and if the tide rises they do not rise with it. They sell for a fantastic price too. People fall for them, leaking deckheads and all. This is the grim side of the houseboat market.

'On the other side you do get some new ones of the luxury flat type that are quite all right.

'No finance company in its right mind would touch the old ones. If anything went wrong they are worth nothing. The other type could be financed from the physical point of view, but there are other difficulties. There is the matter of tenure during the run of the agreement. A chap gets a mooring, then gets slung out with two weeks to quit and nowhere to put the houseboat. He tries to hand it back to the finance company and they don't know what to do with it either. This is the black side of it.'

However, relenting a little, he did add that where the boat was all right and the customer was all right and credit-worthy, and where the run of the agreement as far as moorings were concerned was all right as well, 'we might have a go at it'.

Another such firm said there was only one make of new houseboat they would lend on, if the buyer was credit-worthy. And repayments on a £1,000 advance, over five years, would work out at about £24.15 a month. Their reasons for giving most houseboats a miss were that sitting in stagnant water the boats tended to get a chemical action along the waterline which could cause decay; that sections of woodwork opened up in the sun, then took in rainwater and began to rot; that stagnant water collecting in bilges could cause trouble; that most of these boats were in fresh rather than salt water and this was more inclined to cause decay; and that there was a lack of security of moorings.

However, merchant bankers Cedar Holdings, 60 Pall Mall, London SW1, say that if you want to borrow on your house to buy a houseboat they might consider this arrangement—depending on the value of the house.

If you get around to it, it's a novel life aboard a houseboat, in a world that is gently rocking. You have to get used to being tidy, as in a caravan, with no surplus space; and used to neighbours as varied as the boats themselves— actors, artists, city people—all enjoying this slightly different Wind-in-the-Willowish existence.

Some houseboats can be reached over a gangplank from the pavement. To get to others you have to tramp through muddy fields to a canal; or perhaps climb across the decks of several other craft.

In some houseboats the only addition to the simple built-in furniture may be a vase of plastic flowers. Others may be luxuriously equipped. I was aboard one that had a grand piano. Another had a fireplace and gallery bedroom with the double bed swathed in white fur.

CHAPTER 10

Equipping and letting

Equipping a holiday home for yourself need not be very costly, and it does provide a marvellous excuse to buy new things for your main home and shunt the current TV set or refrigerator down to the cottage.

You can begin collecting furniture bargains in advance of getting your other home, as it's a good idea to have a few things to spread around as soon as you take possession. Bits of furniture and some curtains take away the untenanted look that attracts vandals. If you are going to be working there at weekends before you begin staying, you will be grateful for a few chairs and a table or two when you stop for meals or a rest.

But I am not sure that it is wise to buy major items in advance. For one thing the owner of the place might want to sell some of the furniture, and that could save you trouble and the cost of transport. Moreover, cottage or bungalow may have oddly shaped rooms in which, for instance, a round or rectangular dining table could fit better than a square one. Single beds might leave more circulation space in a small bedroom than a double bed. Indeed a double might not go up a cottage staircase.

If you expect to use the place in winter you will need to furnish more thoroughly. Some carpet and heavier curtains will make it cosier on dark chilly evenings. With really old cottages that have exposed beams beneath upper floors you will hear a good deal of sound as people walk round and you may have to allow for thickish coverings for upstair floors.

If a property is purely for summer use it is better to keep it as labour-saving as possible, unless you are going to employ cleaning help. Polished floors can be quickly swept; flagged or tiled ones can be mopped over. Either will make life easier than carpets if the family is going to be in and out of fields or garden all the time. A few mats will remove the bleakness. Rush matting sold in foot squares for about 15p a piece, is useful. You can buy the minimum and 'sew' on more squares with string if you find you need them.

On the minimum-work theme—don't clutter window ledges and mantelshelves with things that will have to be dusted. If there is a decent timber staircase that will justify staining or polishing, use it without carpeting and save an awkward vacuuming chore. Wooden settles or window seats look right in a cottagey place, and can be spread with cushions; it is easier to wash cushion covers than a complete chair covering when a muddy dog has leapt on them.

Oldish furniture from a saleroom is the obvious choice for a casual holiday place in the country, and blends more suitably than glossy modern stuff. You can watch local papers for sales of house-contents, or there may be an auctioneer in the area who collects furniture for a fortnightly or monthly sale. Even if you can't attend on sale day but see something you like when wandering round his rooms beforehand, he may let you 'put a price' on it and bid up to that amount on your behalf.

Often you can pick up mixed 'lots' of cutlery, garden tools, or bundles of curtains, that will be useful in a holiday home where it doesn't matter if things match or not. You are sure to be able to acquire pictures from salerooms, one or two of which might be bearable on the walls or would serve to cover a smear on the paper. Those with ornate frames could have the picture removed, the frame painted or gilded and a mirror put in—useful in bedrooms. I have seen wide picture frames broken up, made into a continuous piece and used as pelmets.

I remember one auctioneer saying that the best time to get bargains in his room was at the sales nearest to bank holidays. People didn't feel in the mood for buying furniture then and few would turn up, so those who did came away with good value.

Keep an eye on second-hand shops—not the expensive antique variety—and look out for things that can be used for different purposes. Two halves of a round table will make heads for twin beds. I've seen a carved door, on its side, used effectively as the head for a double bed. An intricate pair of antlers, dug out of the dust at the back of the shop, will take any number of towels in a bathroom.

Some shops will keep wardrobe doors with long mirrors, when the rest of the suite has been broken up. If the mirror is in a reasonable state these are useful fixed to bedroom walls—or they give an illusion of space if they are set at the end of a landing. Put on their sides, over a shelf, they make a 'dressing table'. The wood to which they are attached can be improved by painting it to match the wall, or by adding a beading. Always check before making this sort of purchase that there is no sign of woodworm, as that was probably the reason why the rest of the suite was destroyed.

Painting a batch of odd furniture the same colour, and adding matching handles to wardrobe, dressing table and chest of drawers, will link them together a bit more. If you come upon a cheap marble washstand in a junk place, grab it. The marble will make coffee or garden tables, or be a boon in the kitchen for rolling pastry on.

If your second home is the wing of an old house, a rectory, or somewhere with large rooms you may find furnishing a cheaper exercise than you expected. Few people want large old stuff these days and if you have room for it you can buy it at sales much more reasonably than smaller pieces that will fit into modern homes.

Don't forget the white elephant stall at bazaars or fêtes, or the junk stall in the local market. One weekend-home owner picked up a fine brass bedstead at a country market for 10p, and the stallholder gave him a fireguard for nothing, on his agreeing to remove 150 kilner jars that wouldn't sell.

You can often get bundles of dog-eared books for a song from secondhand places, bazaars, jumble sales, or the Oxfam shop, and they are a worthwhile investment. Not only do they fill up shelves and give a room a bit of life, but they can be a godsend on a wet day. Who knows what gem of Victoriana may be found among them to keep a restless child or guest curled up in a chair for hours.

And that's another point. However you get them, do make sure there are sufficient comfortable chairs for everyone to settle down in to watch the second-best TV set, or just to sleep in when the weather drives them indoors.

If you need bedspreads, brightly patterned Indian ones are cheap and wash easily. An extra one or two will make curtains as well.

Firms who equip stands for exhibitions are worth tracking down. You can often buy carpet from them that has been used just for the week or two of the show, and is then sold off at a reduced price.

If the bath that came with your cottage has curving legs and looks grim, don't despair. It will seem much more approachable if you board in the side with horizontal strips of tongued and grooved timber. Or panel it with hardboard and cover the hardboard with cheerful ceramic tiles.

A man with an ordinary little house in the country made a feature of his porch by lining it with different tiles he brought back from holidays abroad. And he asked friends going on similar trips to bring him a tile rather than any other souvenir. His nostalgic porch became quite a talking point.

If you want to furnish your cottage cheaply, tell all your friends about it. You'll be surprised how many will turn out something to give you. I know a hairdresser who regaled her clients for months with a commentary on her cottage hunting and restoring, and when she got to the equipping point they vied with each other in turning out unused articles to help her furnish it.

Bear in mind that if you are going to let, you may want somewhere in which to lock away a few personal things. A small room, or a large cupboard, is the ideal. Failing that, keep some drawers in a bureau for this purpose. One couple I know got an old mahogany desk for 37p from an office-furniture shop that was closing down, and by the time they had replaced the torn leather top with a substitute material and polished the wood, they seriously considered putting it in their main home. Their regret was that they hadn't room in their estate car for the office chair that the shop would have given them free if they could have taken it away at the same time.

This leads to another vital subject. If you are going to be carrying timber, paints, garden implements, bedding, and furniture to and fro while getting your holiday home organised, perhaps over a year or two, it might be worth considering picking up a cheap van. It will save rough wear on your own car and enable you to take, from saleroom to cottage, furniture that would cease to be a bargain if you had to pay for transporting each item.

One cottage owner bought a post office van for this purpose. It was advertised for tender and his low bid got it. Another acquired a redundant ambulance which he found particularly useful as he and his wife used to sleep in it in their cottage garden when major work was being done to the roof of the property.

If you intend to let your holiday home, the most sensible way to furnish is with reasonably solid, not too expensive, but certainly not the cheapest, articles. With poor quality stuff you get a lot of breakages, and if people think an owner hasn't taken any trouble over a place, they may not either. Strong serviceable equipment is the order of the day. People on holiday don't want to be worrying that the child will wreck something that doesn't look very strong. But anything too good is a liability. And in fairness to everyone, lock away any valuable ornaments.

Most owners provide blankets, bedding, crockery and cutlery. The majority do not include linen because of wear and tear, although people from overseas find it a help to have this provided.

It is appreciated if washing machines, washing-up machines, spin dryers, vacuums, irons—anything that makes life easier for the housewife on holiday—can be left in furnished properties along with easily understood instructions on how to use them.

An electric kettle is cheap to provide and gives quite disproportionate pleasure with quick cups of tea available on returning from trips and pressure off the cooker at meal times. An electric toaster will also be appreciated.

Another point with kitchen equipment—don't buy the cheapest saucepans. They will get a lot of use, so choose pans with bases that don't bend under bad treatment.

Deposits can be taken against damage, but many owners don't bother, and say they seldom have any trouble. Most tenants replace anything they break, or leave some money and a note on the kitchen table: 'Sorry, we smashed three plates'. Occasionally you get a real 'shocker', but not often, according to letting agents. One firm said that out of 2,000 bookings they might get eight or nine complaints. But another firm which handles the letting of a large many-storeyed house for an owner who lives elsewhere still remembers a family that moved every item of the heavy furniture to a different floor. The owner was faced with a £25 bill for getting removal men in to put everything back again.

You will have to decide whether or not to have a telephone. In a remote place you will find it useful yourself, and so may tenants. But there are risks. In one furnished property a tenant ran up a bill for £180 with one call. The agents got the money back for the owner, but it took them nine months. It may be better not to tempt fate. You can, if you wish, top up the rent to include an estimated number of calls, but this is hit-and-miss and won't cover the £180 man. It used to be possible on a manual exchange to ask that calls made during a letting period should be charged separately, but nearly all of the country is now on STD. It is possible to get the Post Office to partly lock the mechanism to prevent the dialling of trunk calls. But long conversations on local numbers can also be expensive.

Another suggestion is that you have a plug-in phone and lock it away from tenants if you don't know them well. It only costs another 10p a quarter. But it would be possible for a tenant knowing about the arrangement to bring his

137

own plug-in phone and use it with impunity—to your cost.

Probably the most foolproof system is the coin-box. For this you pay the normal rental for the phone and an extra £10 a year for the coin box (plus a £5 connection charge for installation). From this you get back 30 per cent on the cost of calls made, so if tenants use it very much it is to your advantage.

How do you find tenants? There are several ways of going about it. Tell your friends and people in the office— but if you are going to do it as a business proposition, make it plain from the outset that you charge a market rent. Put cards in shop windows, advertise in local or national news-papers, and the London 'evenings'. Try insertions in annual publications like *Furnished Holiday Homes and Caravans*, and *Self Catering Holidays*, and in *Daltons Weekly. The Lady* is a useful magazine for that sort of advertising. It is read by many people living overseas who need to rent places for longish periods for UK leave.

You can put your property in the hands of letting agents. Not all general estate agents will deal with furnished houses or flats and the attendant work of checking inventories and meters, so you will have to find those who do. A national agency which specialises in this sort of letting is Taylings Holiday Cottages, 28-30 Queens House, Leicester Square, London WC2. They handle about 700 cottages, bungalows, chalets and flats in Britain and Ireland and bring out a list each year, under counties, and with a paragraph about each property. This is compiled from information given by their inspecting officers, and from a form that owners are asked to fill in.

The sort of factual entry they give reads something like this: 'Simple homely cottage with shared garden and park-ing, 3 mins by car to the sea. Sandy beaches within 6 mile radius. Living/dining room. Kitchen with electric cooker. Fridge. WC. Twin-bedroom. Double bedroom. Iron, electric fires, electric water heater. NO BATHROOM. Bus stops by cottage gate. Milk delivered daily from nearby farm, also groceries delivered. Oct-Mar £5.50. Apr-Sept £14.10.'

Rentals are quoted on a weekly basis.

A payment of £2 entitles an owner to an entry in the booklet (20,000 are printed each year for distribution to applicants and to people who booked with them the previous year). Inclusion of a photograph costs a further £2.25. They need details by mid-October for the following year's list which appears in December. But later entries go into the dozen or so supplements that come out up to August of the year concerned.

Every property, except a few in very isolated parts like the Scottish islands, is visited by one of their inspecting officers before they list it. If it has not been inspected this is stated.

They find Devon, Cornwall and Dorset the most popular districts, with Pembrokeshire and Scotland next. Dorset, they say, attracts overseas visitors because they like to feel within reach of London. July and August inevitably produce the highest demand for properties to rent, but the spring bank holiday period and Easter bring plenty of applicants. There is also a certain demand for places in November, mostly from the older people and honeymoon couples.

Rents range from about £14 to £55 a week in August. In winter they are about £5, but most owners do not want the trouble of single-week lettings at this time of year and prefer winter applicants to take a property for three or four weeks.

The type of holiday home that lets best is one sleeping

five or six people, perhaps with a divan in the sitting room. It is detached, near a beach, pleasantly decorated, simply furnished and not over-priced. There is also a fairly heavy demand for away-from-it-all accommodation, 'bumping your way over a mile of track to reach it—at the right rent'.

Taylings ask tenants to fill in a form on leaving and give their comments on a place, so they get a good idea of people's reactions to different types of property.

The first essential is cleanliness. They stress that it is vital to make arrangements for a cleaner to go in before each tenants arrives, or to get cleaning done by some means, even though it is the tenant's obligation to leave the property in good condition.

Pets can be a problem, I was told. People want to take their dog/canary/cat/or other odds and ends. But from the owner's point of view they can spoil furniture, and some stipulate no pets, although the fewer restrictions you put on a property, the better it lets.

The key may be left with a caretaker, in the door, or in the apple tree . . . all owners have their own arrangements. Tenants are advised to bring a torch—presumably in case they have to go hunting for the key late at night in the apple tree. The agents send a final instruction letter to tenants telling them how to find the property—and the key— and other things that the owners think might help, such as the name and address of a shop from which food can be ordered in advance.

Not many owners seem to insure in case, say, a tenant falls down the stairs, but that is something that should be considered. 'We do not know how many owners declare to their insurance companies that they are letting,' said the agents, 'but we think they ought to discuss it with their company.'

Tayling's system is to take a deposit, at the time of book-

Page 141 Two widely contrasting types of Spanish holiday homes:
(above) a villa with a magnificent background of mountains and—
overleaf . . .

Page 142 Flats in Ibiza: less romantic perhaps than the villa but simpler domestic economy

ing, of a third of the amount payable, with a cancellation premium to cover anyone who has to drop out for medical reasons. If an intending tenant cancels for any other reason he is liable for the whole rent (unless he insures against other contingencies or there is re-letting). But these holiday homes are not easy to let again at short notice.

Three weeks before the holiday the tenant must pay the balance, plus any necessary deposit. Taylings add their commission to whatever sum the owner asks for rental, and find it better if rent can be inclusive of gas, electricity, hire of television, allowance for cleaning and anything else for which payment is required.

Usually owners estimate gas and electricity consumption; if one tenant uses more, another will use less, and so it evens out. But some owners prefer to install meters. These agents feel that telephones are not needed and not worth the risk.

The agents send the owner a cheque each month for lettings commenced that month. But they warn owners not to be too optimistic about income. If you bought your cottage cheaply years ago you should get a good percentage return. But with today's higher prices, the return on a recently bought property—if you do not use it yourself during peak letting periods—could work out about 5-8 per cent gross. They feel you would be unwise to pin your hopes on more. And if the property is let for twenty-four weeks in the year, you are doing pretty well.

When owners first get in touch with them, the agents send a set of notes for guidance, based on their experience of problems that can arise. They stress that accuracy of description is vital and that it is much better to mention at the start anything that could affect a holiday adversely. If there are steep stairs, a bad approach road, ponds or streams that could be dangerous for children, or bunk beds,

143

J

then tell people beforehand. It is better to under-describe the merits of a property than to over-describe and disappoint people. If a place is simple, say so. Many prefer that for a holiday.

Owners should accept bookings promptly and never be surprised at short-notice applications. Every year there are many bookings made at less than a week's notice. They should also give clear directions on how to find the place. No one wants to spend an hour at the end of a tiring journey trying to track down an isolated cottage.

Winter bookings are increasing though tenants expect to pay low rents, and it might be an advantage to have a property occupied at this time even at a nominal rent. But if it is old, damp or not properly heated it is better not to offer it for winter letting.

Particularly important if you are letting during winter, though an obvious precaution at any time, is to leave simple instructions on what to do if there is a burst pipe. Fix them somewhere easily visible and where they won't get lost. You will, if you are wise, familiarise yourself with the plumbing arrangements as soon as you take over the property. Find out where the stop tap is (where water enters the house) and what parts of the system are controlled by other out-of-the-way taps. Make sure they can easily be turned off and on. Label them, saying what they do.

If the house is to be left unoccupied and unheated for periods in cold weather it will be safest to drain the water supply by turning off the main stop tap and opening all hot and cold water taps. Leave them open. When water has ceased running, flush the lavatories.

Open also the draining taps on the boiler and hot water storage cylinder, first making quite sure there is no water-heating system still on. Turn off gas and electricity at the mains. As hot water systems differ a good deal it would be sensible to have a word with a plumber on the correct way of emptying and restarting yours.

Ensure that the water system is properly lagged to prevent freezing if the water is not drained. Pipes in the roof space or in exposed positions can be wrapped in hair felt tied with string or wire. The tank in the roof can be lagged with hair felt, or stramit board. Or box it in, leaving a 3in space all round to be filled with some insulating material like vermiculite or even sawdust. Put a board over the top, with a hole through which vent pipes can discharge into the tank. Do not insulate beneath the tank or you will lose the benefit of any warmth coming up from the house. Try to stop excessive draughts on the tank or pipes.

Most water boards will let you have a leaflet on protecting systems in cold weather. Or the National Federation of Plumbers and Domestic Heating Engineers, 6 Gate Street, London WC2 will send one. Enclose a stamped addressed envelope with your request.

It is important that there should be someone a tenant can get in touch with on arrival if anything is wrong. Leave the person's name, address and phone number—again where it won't be destroyed or lost—together with those of a doctor, plumber, tradesmen, cleaning woman and baby sitters, if any.

Some owners go to the trouble of leaving typed or handwritten 'booklets' with directions on how to cope in all kinds of contingencies, hints on interesting places to visit, shops and cafés offering the best service, details about tradesmen who call and their times. Tenants who are strangers to an area greatly appreciate this sort of assistance. The well-thumbed state of your 'booklet' will soon give you an idea of how often they resort to it.

If you receive rent for letting your holiday home, tax will be payable on this income as on any other. But expenditure on maintenance and repairs—though only so far as relates to the letting—can be allowed as a deduction in computing taxable income.

Elaborating on this, the authorities say that the expenditure which can be allowed consists broadly of normal expenses on maintenance, repairs, insurance and management of property.

'But so far as casual letting is concerned, expenditure on maintenance and repairs to a property which is occupied is allowable as a deduction only if the dilapidation which necessitated the work occurred during a period in which the property was let. In cases of casual letting the deduction for expenditure, if any, will depend very much on the circumstances, and will be a matter for discussion with the taxpayer's inspector.'

CHAPTER 11

The overseas world

The overseas second-home market is a growing one. Bed-sitter 'studio' flats, larger apartments, villas, converted farmhouses and, of course, plots on which to build to your own needs, are offered by countless British agents on the UK market and more British people than you might imagine own such properties.

Spain and the Balearic islands head the popularity polls, and have done right from early postwar years when more and more people began to go there for cheap overseas holidays and found they could buy a little place in a fishing resort for next to nothing. Of course those days didn't last long. The agents and the developers moved in and the concrete jungles of the Costa del Sol were created.

Inevitably there followed the stories of disillusionment: land sold by people who did not own it; blocks of flats that never got built; flats in which cracks appeared before the paint was dry; 'wonderful' sites, bought unseen, that turned out to be swamp or desertland, or next to an airport, or to have no services nor any chance of getting them.

Now the market has settled down, although it is always a

changing one for political and other reasons, and subject to short-lived scares which may make today's good buy seem temporarily a bad one.

The Gibraltar situation has at times, overshadowed the sales of Spanish property to the British, but buyers have learned to live with it and not to worry. Malta has had its ups and downs as prices rushed ahead too fast, then questions of capital gains and estate duty loomed up and set buyers wondering. The Bahamas have had political changes that have reduced their monetary attraction to some purchasers. There have occasionally been question marks over Portugal. The rising and falling premium (payable when buying out of the sterling area) has also affected the overseas market.

But these difficulties come and go and people who have made up their minds to get their own corner in the sun for the most part go ahead and ignore them.

Agents find that purchasers give more thought to what they buy these days and no longer snap up the first thing offered. Many make use of the property inspection tours run by developers and agents. These short, economically priced flights enable people to see for themselves what is offered and often the cost of the trip is refunded if they buy.

Many prospective buyers go on several such tours before they decide, or they may arrange to visit developments while on holiday. Some stay in the overseas holiday home of a friend or relative, and decide then to get something similar. Agents find that a lot of their sales come about in this snowball fashion.

The growing popularity of air travel, with cheap night and charter flights, has helped the sun-homes market. The number of airports is steadily increasing, bringing more areas within reach of the UK. For anyone living near Heathrow, Gatwick or one of the many smaller airports, the two-hour flight to Spain may put a holiday home there within much quicker reach than one in Cornwall or Scotland.

It is surprising what a cross-section of people have bought properties abroad. Garage owners, doctors, singers, bankers, scrap-metal dealers, widows, secretaries, pilots, publicans and publishers—I've met them going out to check on progress of a place they were having built, tanning on the balcony of their flat, or solicitously watering the lemon tree in their newly made garden.

Although prices have risen since the early days of this type of overseas buying you can still get a flat in Spain for £1,400 or a villa for about £2,500 (although you would be wise to pay more), so it is not a world reserved for surtax payers. And there are ways of group buying which can get you into the swim at much lower figures than these.

A lot of the rules that apply to buying at home are just as relevant when it comes to looking for a holiday home abroad.

The chances are you will want to make some use of an overseas place to get away from the British winter, perhaps at Christmas, or for an early holiday. But a good many Mediterranean spots can be cold, windy and wet out of season, though not for as long a period as our winter. They can also be exceedingly dull when hotels are closed and boutiques, and potteries, discothèques and pavement bars are shut until Easter.

On the other hand some of the most popular spots can be too full and noisy for comfort at the height of the season. And remember, in a place where everyone has windows open day and night and sits chattering at sidewalk cafés until the early hours, noise can be a bigger problem than in this country.

A high percentage of people who buy holiday flats abroad do so with the idea of retiring to the area later; perhaps,

149

if the place comes up to their expectations, living in the flat at the start of retirement while supervising the building of a more suitable villa nearby. Retiring abroad can have tax advantages. But the enemy seems to be boredom, and a villa with a garden offers more interest.

You cannot expect luxury at rock-bottom prices. Aim some way above them if you want a property that is well built, well situated and has extra touches in the way of attractive interior tiling, fittings and doors. Make sure that the price you are asked for a plot includes the laying of water, electricity and roadway to it.

Water supply is vital, particularly if you are considering an island or isolated area. There are areas where water can be uncomfortably short in the dry season and though the locals may serenely accept its delivery by carrier—perhaps donkey drawn—the British newcomer might feel less happy about this sort of supply.

Completion dates are a headache with builders the world over. If you are hundreds of miles away you can be sure that your man will be busily finishing off a villa for someone on the spot and not pressing on with yours. So don't rely on promised dates. If you must have occupation by a certain time, try and arrange for a member of your family to stay out there, breathing down his neck. Or ask some British resident to do it for you. And don't believe anyone who says there can't be a tower block built in front of your site. It is quite possible that when you return next year you will find it going up.

Your safest bet is to buy your plot or property through a long-established British estate agent, who is not likely to risk his reputation selling anything he knows to be dubious, and who will have looked into things like ownership, planning and military permission, and plots being fully serviced, before he starts selling.

It won't hurt to ask if his firm has any personal involvement with a development you are considering—and to ask locally about it (word soon gets round). This may not matter, but it is as well to know.

It is essential to make sure about title. Buying land overseas can be tricky if you are dealing with an apparent owner. It is often the custom for a property to be left jointly to all the children of a family. You may find that the piece which interests you has any number of owners scattered all over the world, all of whom will have to consent to the sale in writing before you can legally purchase.

Don't hope to buy with a mortgage outside the sterling area. This is practically impossible under the Exchange Control regulations, which you will keep coming across if you are intending to buy abroad.

Remember that if you buy on an estate—an 'urbanization' you will often find it called—that is being well advertised and promoted, you may not find it too easy to resell an individual property there later. Many British agents are not interested in selling single overseas properties, and local firms may not be very successful in finding buyers in what may be a 'British colony', and perhaps overpriced by their standards. Not everyone makes a handsome profit on such sales. Some certainly do, but you probably won't hear about those who settled for a loss.

Try and make sure, if you are buying a plot, that it is on an estate that will be developed within a reasonable time. British purchasers of land outside the sterling area must undertake to build on it within eighteen months, under our Exchange Control regulations, but that does not apply to other nationalities, or in sterling areas. (In theory you are actually required to complete building within eighteen months, but the Bank of England, which administers the regulations, will make allowances when a builder falls

151

behind schedule.)

If many of your fellow buyers are small-time speculators, hoping to hold their land for a few years and sell at a profit, the unfinished look of the estate will keep down its value and the value of your villa with it. Some developers stipulate that buyers must build within a certain period, to stop this.

Often buyers find that promised swimming pools and shops on developments take longer to appear than they expected. The builder, short of money, has to wait until he can sell more properties in order to finance these developments, or perhaps he has to find someone willing to lease the shops. But early buyers will normally have bought at lower prices than those who come later when the amenities are there.

A man who bought a farmhouse in Malta, improved it and let to a holidaymaker, only to find that his tenant went along to the authorities, got the rent reduced and then refused to leave. Too late he discovered that there was a law, similar to British legislation, which fixed rent levels of a certain type of property, and protected tenants.

Occasionally people have bought in proposed overseas developments, and learned that planning permission to build was not available—or that the developers had disappeared. Almost always these purchases will have been from mushroom firms and not through reputable agents. And probably the prices asked will have been so low that on serious consideration it should have been obvious that the figures were not realistic.

I have talked to dozens of people who have bought second homes abroad. Their experiences have varied and they have had their little grouses. But most have been well satisfied with their purchases. Some, one sensed, were even slightly pleased with themselves for having done something as daring as buying in another country, which certainly put them one up on their neighbours.

One cannot help feeling that those who did regret their deals had themselves to blame, to some extent, for not making enough enquiries at the outset. Every country has its own procedures, but a British agent with an established overseas department should be able to explain the rules of property buying in the part of the world that interests you. Many agents specialise in certain areas, and will, naturally, be most knowledgeable about those.

Overseas countries split into two sections—the sterling areas (or scheduled territories) and non-sterling areas. Into the sterling section come most of the Commonwealth countries. For the purposes of second-home owning one might think in terms of Malta, Gibraltar and Cyprus and, further afield, Bermuda, the Bahamas, British Virgin Islands and other parts of the West Indies; and latterly, with the airport opened in 1971, the Seychelles in the Indian Ocean.

If you want to buy outside the sterling area you must comply with the Exchange Control regulations. Under these, residents of the UK must get permission from the Bank of England for such a purchase, which must be made in investment currency.

You have to buy this currency at the going rate, which might be between 15 and 25 per cent, and add that percentage to the cost of your property. Your bank, brokers, or agents dealing with the property will tell you what the current rate is. and it is quoted regularly in the *Daily Telegraph* as the 'dollar premium' (though it is generally referred to as the 'property dollar').

You are only allowed one non-sterling area property per family. But there is no ruling about price. So while you would not be allowed to buy two flats at £3,000 each, you could buy one house for £6,000. If you plan to retire over-seas and thus emigrate, you are allowed to take £5,000 out, free of the dollar premium.

If you have decided to buy a property in a non-sterling area, get your bank manager to seek permission from the Bank of England. They will want to know such things as the address of the property, total cost, legal charges, a description of the accommodation, furnishings, local taxes, any amounts that will be necessary for repairs, and the name and address of the person selling. Your bank will ultimately obtain the currency for you.

Occasionally you may be offered a property for sterling in a non-sterling country. This will be because a British owner is selling and will accept sterling in payment. It might look as if, buying this way, you will be saving the premium. But, in fact, the price usually takes the premium into account. Even though payment is made in sterling, you must still get Bank of England permission for the purchase.

You might ask what is to stop you lumping the money into a suitcase and taking it abroad, and not worrying about the premium. You can do this, if you like to break the law, or you can find other illegal ways of by-passing the premium. It is no secret that people do. But Treasury investigators keep an eye on what is going on, and they can get on the track of such deals when a property is sold again. Law-breakers risk fines up to three times the amount they seek to evade, or imprisonment.

When it comes to maintaining a non-sterling area home, you are allowed to transfer money to pay things like rates, electricity bills, wages of a caretaker or gardener, free of premium. If you have work done to the building, cash for actual repairs can be taken out premium-free, but not for improvement. In the delightful way an official put it: 'having acquired a property it becomes a British asset and has to be kept up to scratch'. So, maintenance is on one side of the fence, improvement the other. The roof of your British asset collapses and you can use premium-free money to have it repaired. But if you decide to have a new one put on before it falls about your ears, that might be regarded as an improvement, to the cost of which you would have to add the premium.

If you are going to let your overseas home you might as well do it advantageously. You will have to cope with the same problems as letting at home, plus a few more. But you will have better weather and a longer letting season on your side.

A lot of people let to friends, and friends of friends. Even strangers who reply to your advertisements will appreciate being able to ring up and chat about the accommodation and district. How you advertise is up to you. You can put cards in shop windows and a few lines in local papers quite cheaply. If you advertise in the personal or holiday columns of national papers it can be expensive but will reach a much wider public. Timing is important. Some people find January and early autumn are the best times, when people are planning summer and winter holidays.

Have plenty of information written out about the apartment or villa, and what there is to do in the area, how far it is from sea and airport, and send it to applicants, preferably with a photograph. If they decide to rent they will want further information: about car-hire, about shops, which restaurants to go to, how to obtain bottled gas for cooking, and so on.

You will certainly need an agent at the other end to see to maintenance, cleaning, linen-changing and replacements, unless the caretaker in a block of flats or a local person will undertake this. People may also need to be met

155

from planes and to have food left for them.

Apartments let more easily than villas and are less of a liability. Buy in a resort that is not too far from an airport, and if you are clever find one that is popular with low-price Scandinavian tours which bring their people in all through the year and provide greater opportunities for winter letting.

You will usually do better in an area where hotel accommodation is limited. Although if your property is near an hotel you might be able to let to the hotel for overspill guests.

Choose your flat in a block that has a management service. Remember that while you may prefer solitude the average holidaymaker likes plenty of life and eating places round him, and if he is staying in a flat or villa, will want a supermarket nearby for stocking up for breakfasts. He will want to be as close to a beach as possible. (A busy main road between a block of flats and the sea can be a disadvantage, particularly for families with children.)

The thing that is likely to put up the cost of a family's visit to your property, and put them off, is the scheduled air fare. On a package tour arranged by a holiday firm they would generally go by charter flight, which would cost much less and make their total holiday cheaper than the stay at your accommodation, even if they do their own catering.

The way of overcoming this is to join one of the group schemes which allow owners to charter aircraft for people holidaying in their property. Owners' Services Limited, Broxbourne, Hertfordshire, do this for members, and a good deal more. They have over 7,000 people on their books, whose property they let. Most of the properties are in Spain and the Balearic islands, but there are some also in Malta, Portugal, Corfu and Cyprus.

An owner belonging to such an organisation is able to use the charter services himself when he goes to his apartment for his own holidays.

OSL was started by an overseas property owner who, noting the scheduled-flight obstacle to letting his Majorca apartment, got a group of others to join him in chartering an aircraft for holiday tenants. The idea worked well and, with his firm backing him, he switched entirely to arranging this service for owners.

It soon became apparent that there were more ways in which owners could be helped, and the organisation try to deal with them all. They produce holiday apartment and villa brochures, advertise and make the holiday arrangements. They handle management, cleaning, leaving of food parcels, rent collecting, inventories. They see tenants in, fix maid service and hire cars. They will furnish apartments and make replacements. They also run an estate agency.

It occurred to them that the know-how they were gathering about the holiday-home market could be put to everyone's benefit. So they are now building apartments for sale to people who can, if they wish, let through the organisation. Their contention is that, having found where people most like to holiday abroad, the type and size of place they want and the facilities needed, they can build to give the holidaymaker exactly what he wants. Therefore the person who buys one of these apartments should stand a good chance of letting profitably.

A point that concerns families when they spend part of each year abroad is how they are to pay for medical treatment if the need arises. A private patients' insurance scheme is the answer. The British United Provident Association, 25 Essex Street, London WC2, say that British residents who subscribe to their scheme are covered while abroad, if they are not in another country for more than six

157

months in a year. The London Association for Hospital Services, Tavistock House South, Tavistock Square, London WC1, has schemes entitling members to treatment anywhere in the world, with subscriptions based on benefits obtainable. Incidentally, I have talked with overseas home owners who have had medical treatment abroad, and found that they have usually been well satisfied with it.

An apartment in a newly built block, often with a swimming pool for residents—for which there will be an annual maintenance charge—is probably the most typical choice for a holiday home in the sun. The range goes from 'studio' type—one room with sleeping accommodation, kitchen and bathroom—to lush and expensive penthouses with numerous rooms and one or two terraces. Sometimes they are sold furnished. Some blocks have maid service, and restaurants, bars, supermarkets, hairdressers and a letting office.

The next most popular way of getting an overseas home is to buy a plot on an estate and choose from one of several villa designs, which the developer will build for you. Plots may be pocket-handkerchief size to ten acres or more. Sometimes you are offered serviced plots (with roads, drainage, water and electricity laid on), and you find your own architect and builder.

The other possibility is to buy an individual plot and go the whole way on your own, making sure about planning permission, services and everything yourself. You can use a local architect and builder, or you might import a system-designed house from UK.

There are all sorts of planned developments, geared to the holiday buyer. These vary enormously, depending on what you are prepared to pay, but also on the country and its planning regulations, and on the developer. You may have houses dotted round pinewoods or down hillsides,

Page 159 Majorca: *(above)* view from the balcony of a flat in Canyamel; *(below)* interior of a flat let through Owners Services Ltd

Page 160   *(above)* These unusual pyramid style apartment blocks at
La Grande Motte have become a landmark in this new holiday resort
being built in the south of France; *(below)* your holiday home at
Treasure Cay, Bahamas, could have a 'beach hat' roof with a verandah effect

built along canals, or clustered in modern 'villages', copying the local architecture. They are frequently near a beach. If they are inland they are generally built with retirement buyers particularly in mind.

There is usually a clubhouse with restaurant, forming a centre. Often this was originally a farmhouse, the developer having bought the surrounding land from a departing farmer. There will probably be a swimming pool and supermarket, and there may be some letting arrangement. But facilities may vary from nothing at all—or promised but not materialised—to golf courses, riding clubs, sailing, polo, even flying clubs.

If you know a country well and can speak the language, buying your individual plot and arranging everything yourself should be the most economical method of getting your second home—provided you can be around to supervise the builder or get someone else to do it for you.

Or you might go halfway and cut out the middleman's profit by choosing a plot and villa design on an estate. But you won't exactly be 'away from it all' that way. Some estates get very closely built on. Some don't. Some get sold almost entirely to British families and become almost 'colonies'. Some are sold to all nationalities.

The other alternative is to buy an existing property either to move right into, or to modernise. An old terrace house in an unfashionable fishing village, or an inland cottage or farmhouse can still be picked up cheaply enough, possibly for just over £1,000; in some cases for less. But you will have to spend £2,000 or £3,000 modernising it.

You can also get windmills and watermills, presbyteries or minor castles to convert if you feel like taking them on.

One thing to remember is not to use the same yardstick for choosing a home as one might in Britain. You will live to regret big picture windows or a shelterless sun roof in a

161

country where the sun blazes down all day. Small windows that can be shuttered to keep out the heat, deep arched shady balconies and terraces, high cool-floored rooms and gardens with shady foliage are the order of the day. There is no need to worry about a garage, but a carport in which to keep the car out of the sun is useful. Terraces are more important than dining rooms; if you have air-conditioning you want it in the bedroom, for if it is very hot you aren't likely to be indoors in a sitting room much, to need it there.

A swimming pool is well worth considering if you have space. It may cost £1,000, but prices vary with size and country. Even the hottest region has its cold and wet spells —so some form of heating may be more useful than you imagine.

In Mediterranean countries houses are often private and inward looking—high-walled, shuttered, perhaps even seeming ill-cared for from the outside. But don't let that put you off. Inside you may find interior courtyards, fine stone staircases, beautifully proportioned rooms and an elegance of design that you could not have suspected from the almost shabby face they show to the public.

With the world to choose from, finding the most suitable spot for your overseas hideaway may not be easy. If you care you can use a process of elimination, working through how much you can afford, fares, time available for travelling; whether you like the people, their food and their politics. Do you like islands, or do they make you feel hemmed in? Do you want tourists around—and the British—or do you want to be miles away from both? Do you like flat land or mountainous? Can you bear it being very hot at times? Will you want to swim, sail, climb, play golf? Do you want a place that will always have some greenery, or don't you mind everything being brown and baked in August? Must you have miles of beach or will you swim from the rocks?

Alternatively you can be the person whose method of choice is explained as: 'Well, my wife and I were on holiday and we saw this cottage...'

Taking a quick glance at specific areas, Spain is first choice with the British, with thousands actually resident, apart from owning holiday properties there. It offers the least expensive homes, has highly developed holiday areas like the Costa del Sol and the Costa Brava that become full of tourists, but by keeping a few miles away from the coast you can avoid the throng.

There are dozens of schemes in which to buy property, from the far south around Gibraltar to the foothills of the Pyrenees. You can get apartments from about £1,400, villas with land from well under £3,000, country cottages for modernisation from £1,800. There are also joint buying schemes under which you could own a furnished apartment for a month every year in perpetuity for £325 upwards.

The Almeria district is one that is becoming popular with developers of late. And the area around Javea is a good one for improved or improvable cottages. There are various lease-back schemes in different developments through which you may be offered 10 to 15 per cent a year of the cost of a property, through letting. (But you may find that the higher the guaranteed income is, the higher the original cost of the property).

Next in popularity come the Balearic islands of Majorca, Menorca and Ibiza—Majorca topping the poll with property buyers as well as tourists. It offers most interest and a selection of developments, though not the cheapest. As it is the largest island it gives the best opportunities for letting, and like the others it has direct air links with UK.

Typical—as against cheapest—prices in Majorca might be: for a villa site of one-fifth of an acre, on the coast or

163

with an unobstructed view of the sea, and fully serviced, £7,000; for a 900sq ft apartment, two bedrooms, close to the sea, £6,500.

Menorca, next in size, greenest and least sophisticated, still delights in reminding you of the days when Nelson was there. Several developments vie with each other in offering bargains and prices are very reasonable.

Ibiza is quaint in parts, modern in others, and its hippy colony has achieved notoriety. Some of its coves provide attractive settings for secluded developments of apartments suitable for holidays or retirement.

Malta, in the sterling area, has had the British there so long that it hardly seems a foreign place. The old parts are interesting and the winters are warm. Everyone understands English and with the increase in numbers of hotels in recent years it has overcome the egg-and-chips image left over from its long spell of catering for the services.

But it is flat and dried up in summer. It is the sort of place you either like or don't like. It is not strong on beaches. The neighbouring island of Gozo, reached by ferry, offers more attractive scenery.

Most of the property on the Maltese islands is offered on a perpetual leasehold because much of the land is owned by the Church. To anyone interested in buying, Malta is something of a problem area, the change of government in 1971 making its future plans uncertain. The £50 travel limit sent people flocking to the island and the property market boomed. Prices rose astronomically. Then there were financial scares, which eventually sorted themselves out.

At the time of writing the 4,000 or so British residents, who only pay local income tax at 2½p in the £ if they have pensions over £1,400, still enjoy life and property buyers are taking advantage of falling prices. You can get one-

fifth of an acre with a sea view for £3,000, a coastal apartment for £6,000, or you can buy inland for much less. You
can also get bank loans for up to fifteen years.

Malta Tourist Office, 24 Haymarket, London SW1, can
supply a useful book about living in Malta.

Portugal really means the Algarve region in the south for
most British buyers—an area of splendid beaches, a feeling
of open space, thousands of almond trees blossoming like
snow in the spring, and of villas rather than tower blocks.
Agents say the typical buyer is likely to live in the country
at home, and to be fairly well off.

You might get beach club houses, with three bedrooms
and two bathrooms, selling around £9,000, or smaller places
at £5,500. A good quality house on a quarter-acre site with
swimming pool might be £12,000. Or you could have a
rather special home built, with retirement in view, on a
two-and-a-half to ten-acre site costing up to £20,000 with
land.

Portugal is not cheap. But it has tight planning control,
which residents like, and the Algarve people are charming.

France is coming back in the property market 'possibles'
for British buyers, after years when prices have been too
high to be considered by the ordinary person. Now marina
developments in the south are providing apartments at
£6,000 and less. There is also the major government-backed
Languedoc/Roussillon project on 110 miles of the Mediterranean coast north-east of Spain. Here six new resorts, one
being developed to a pyramid theme, are being built between existing ones, and thousands of properties are being
sold from about £3,000 to £20,000. This is a Mecca of holiday homes, but mostly it is the French themselves who are
buying.

There are also inland farmhouses, which have become
fashionable in recent years, for British buyers to take over

and modernise, perhaps paying £1,500 or so for the original building and land. They make marvellous places for children to run wild in during summer holidays—and as France is not far they can be bundled there in a car without the high cost of air fares.

But you have to pick your farmhouse. Some can be isolated and grim: as one woman put it, 'Talk about Cold Comfort Farm.' A Briton owning one of these farms has been watching agents buying up properties around him and offering them at double the price. 'Everyone', he said, 'is falling over themselves at the favourite pastime of doing the British.' Even so, I have heard delightful stories of co-operation and friendliness.

Cyprus has certainly had its political troubles, but if the memory of these is allowed to fade and tourism increases it should become a popular place for second homes. True, it is rather far away, but, if you have retirement in view, it offers attractive mountain and coastal scenery, and a considerable British community.

It is in the sterling area, but prices are not low. The Cypriots themselves have always been active land buyers, which keeps levels up. You might get sites from £1,500, flats from £4,500—but more often £6,000—and villas from £6,000-£8,000. Of course if you like to go up into the mountains you get into a different range of prices: sites from £400 and village houses from about £900 (with £2,000 to be spent on them).

Not much is offered in Italy through British agents—just individual old houses in the north and at quite high figures, though there were a few for modernisation starting at £3,500. One agent recently had a complete—but derelict —village going near Domodossala. It fetched £5,000. But the motorways are opening up new areas and more seems gradually to be coming into the British buyer's price range.

Other areas you could consider are Sardinia—highly priced villas and plots in jet-set schemes here; Elba, with some existing apartments to be had; Corsica, where there is a little development; Gibraltar, with apartments; Tunisia—showing signs of popularly priced developments. There were round-roofed holiday villas there at £1,500. But some British owners discovered that it took up to eighteen months to get their deeds, which can be awkward if you want to sell again quickly.

There is again some choice of individual villas in the Greek islands, after years when nothing has been available to us. But in Corfu, for instance, foreigners cannot own property, so you have either to buy through a Greek nominee or form a company.

If you prefer mountains, you can buy a plot and build a chalet in Andorra, or there are apartments to be had in at least one development in a Swiss ski resort—prices from £2,500. But the Swiss do not normally encourage foreign buyers.

We are not finished yet. A little estate property is to be had in Madeira, and a lot in the Canaries, both on the principal islands and on the odd, volcanic Lanzarote with its moonscape scenery. The islands are warm, Spanish, inexpensive, and much visited by the British.

The Seychelles in the Indian Ocean are of limited interest but with a new international airport, they have come on to the map. They are in the sterling section, and are very lovely. If they should become a popular holiday area (a fortnight's holiday on one of the islands can be had for £193) land prices can only rise. At the moment, with little hotel accommodation, anyone with property to let can hardly fail to profit. One British agent has a selection of houses and land available.

Across the Atlantic you have Bermuda, the Bahamas and

167

West Indies, for people with money to spend on high air fares, high property prices and high cost of living. But high rents are to be had, too, from Americans. It is a sterling area so there is no premium to find, and there are all sorts of tax benefits.

The beaches are of fine white powdery sand, the sea around the islands is transparent, and you have as much sunshine as you will get anywhere in the world. But there are political shadows to be reckoned with as the islands move towards greater independence.

Many of the Bahamas developments are of the resort type. You buy a plot in an area devoted entirely to golf, sailing, snorkling and the pursuit of leisure. You get a little house with a roof like a beach hat built on it. It may cost you something like £17,000—much more if it stands in the banana trees and looks out at a sea smooth as blue enamel. Or you can buy an apartment with bronze tinted glass to keep out the sun, or a town marina house on a canal, with steps down to your boat.

It is all pricey, but there are letting and lease-back arrangements whereby rents will help you buy your property over a period. One Bahamas scheme promises buyers exchange holidays in similar developments in Switzerland, France and Mexico. The Bahamas Commission, 39 Pall Mall, London SW1 can advise on agents and developers.

Agents for other countries advertise in the property pages of the national press, and in the magazine *Homes Overseas*.

Index

Index

170